NUGGETS OF GOLD

To Soothe Your Soul

An Inspired Collection of Original
Poems and Stories to Warm Your Heart
and Lift Your Spirit

By Travis Jenkins

Dedication

This book is dedicated to all of you, my friends, and brothers and sisters in Christ. I pray you feel welcomed and encouraged as you ponder, meditate, and enjoy the poems and stories in this book. You will notice on many occasions as you make your way through each chapter that I refer to you as my friend. It is my hope that by the time you finish reading these writings, you will consider me, on some level, your friend, as well. Most of all, I pray you will either strengthen your relationship, or start a new relationship with Jesus, and He will be your friend, too – your best friend.

Meet the Poet

Poetry found me.

One day, while I was in college, I saw an advertisement in our local paper for a poetry contest. I'm not really sure what inspired me or motivated me, but I read that advertisement and said, "I'm going to write a poem and enter.I don't recall what came of that poetry contest or my entry, but decades later, God is resurrecting my love for writing to make a difference today. It is never too late for God to use anything. God called me to start utilizing my gifts, forming my words, and pouring out His messages of hope for others. I made myself available, and God has been blessing me ever since.I hope that through my poetry, others, like yourself, can find hope in Jesus and drown out the noise of the devil.

While putting the finishing touches on my book *Christian Rhymes for Trying Times,* I encountered a "God moment." God not only prompted me to take the hundreds of poems He had recently inspired, but He gave me a title and a vision for a cover. What follows is a poem God inspired that tells the story of my writing relationship with Him. God has really touched my heart through the writing of this book and I pray you find it a blessing as well.

Nuggets from Heaven

Gold nuggets of God from heaven
flowing down to soothe my soul,
I must pass them on to you, my friend,
for God said this was my role.
I do not fully understand this miracle,
but I no longer find it odd,
I know the words I share with you
are awe-inspired by God.
The nuggets fall from heaven's door,
and are burned into my heart,
The spirit tells me what I should write,
and it's up to me to do my part.
Don't get confused and think these nuggets
are as important as God's Word,
Yet realize they were inspired by God,
and it's a message that should be heard.
God worked on me for many years
to get me where I could hear,
I was busy satisfying selfish needs,
and living a life of doubt and fear.
The nuggets of gold in God's Holy Word
helped turn my life around,
If you want true nuggets of gold, my friend,
God's Word is where they're found.
Still, God works in mysterious ways,
and sometimes it is us He can use,
He doesn't always bang us on the head
He often leaves subtle clues.
I believe that's what happened to me

with the writing talent I possess,
God put some subtle clues in my path,
and I was scared I must confess.
But God gave me a picture so perfectly clear,
and it came with definite goals,
I saw nuggets from heaven inspiring me,
and I saw Jesus saving lost souls.
So, here I am with nuggets from heaven
God flowed them down to me
I'm doing my part by passing them along
to help God set the lost souls free.

Dear Reader,

I am excited and blessed to be before you once again to share poems and stories inspired through my personal relationship with Christ Jesus. I was truly amazed at the response I received for my first book, *Christian Rhymes for Trying Times*. If you somehow missed it, I encourage you to get your copy, available on Amazon.com, and share your thoughts with me.

While I was going through the publishing and printing process of my first book, God inspired me with well over one hundred new poems and stories. I had no intention of writing a second book, but God had a different plan. The purpose of both books is to show the importance of God in our everyday life, but this book is a bit different than my first book. Both are centered on God the Father, and God the Son, however, there are some stories and poems that address other subjects and are just plain fun to read.

I hope you find this book fun and interesting, yet also helpful and inspiring. Most of all, I pray you find yourself drawn into meaningful thought as to where you are in your walk with Christ. We are made to love, worship, share, and glorify God. While the process is similar, the picture looks different for each of us as we seek to do God's will in and through our life. If you feel you've drifted away from God, just know He still loves you and His arms are open wide to welcome you back into the fold. If you feel strong in the Lord, my desire is to encourage you to continue to grow in your love for Jesus, and to develop a passion to share Him with others.

As you contemplate each poem, may God inspire you with the thoughts and ideas that will strengthen your relationship with Him.

I beseech you therefore, brethren, by the mercies of God, that ye present your bodies a living sacrifice, holy, acceptable unto God, which is your reasonable service. And be not conformed to this world; but be ye transformed by the renewing of your mind, that ye may prove what is the good, and acceptable, and perfect will of God.

—Romans 12: 1-2

Table of Contents

Section One

THINK ABOUT IT

For Reflection:

A common thing I hear people say is, "I've never thought about it." Well, you need to, and here's your chance.

Finally, brethren, whatsoever things are true, whatsoever things are honest, whatsoever things are just, whatsoever things are pure, whatsoever things are lovely, whatsoever things are of good report; if there be any virtue, and if there be any praise, think on these things.

—Philippians 4: 8

Think About It

A Helping Hand

Life is but a journey and we know not where it ends,
Along the way we share good times with all our special friends.
Though we may be true to our self, a special need is there,
To share our love with others, and to see that others care.
Each of us choose different things to give our life its blend,
The common thread we all choose, is to share it with a friend.
Life is tough, we get down, and sometimes don't understand,
That's when we look to our friends to lend a helping hand.
You may think you're strong and your life is etched in stone,
Still, the best of folks fail, when they venture on their own.
God's design I'm quite sure, there really is no doubt,
Was to put people on this earth to help each other out.
So, remember as you live life and venture along your way,
God's design from long ago still holds true for today.
Friends are people put in your path God wants you to meet,
And the friendships of your journey help make your
life complete.

A Speck of Sand

As I stare off into the cosmos
I feel like a tiny speck of sand,
How I can be so small and have such purpose
Is awfully hard to understand.
Sometimes I feel I'm useless
yet, I trust God has a plan,
I know I can always count on Him
so, I hold tightly to His hand.
Still, my head spins around
trying to figure my life out,
Why God put me in this giant cosmos
and what this journey's all about.
It's awesome knowing God will use me,
and He lives deep in my soul,
But, it's hard to grasp how this speck of sand
can play such an important role.
You may think I should rethink this thing
and I'm not as important as I seem,
But, I tell you friend I'm mighty important
because I have Jesus on my team.
You heard me right, I didn't stutter
That's exactly what I said,
I play an important role on Team Jesus
I go wherever I am led.
Still, sometimes I feel so insignificant
like just a tiny speck of sand,
I'm hardly even noticeable to anyone
on this massive chunk of land.
But God sees me and knows my purpose

He has a specific role for me to play,
It's okay to feel a little lost
as I journey along life's way.
For the cosmos is a mighty big place
and I'm only an ordinary man,
God understands if sometimes I feel
like just a tiny speck of sand.
Perhaps you feel this way at times,
going through your own personal life,
Your just a speck of sand, in a great big land
dealing with your daily strife.
Don't lose hope, God has a purpose for you,
you're more important than it may seem,
Though just a speck of sand, God has a plan
if you'll let Jesus lead your team.
Oh, you'll feel lost at times, my friend,
but you'll be a totally different man,
You'll realize you have a purpose
and that life can be quite grand.
You'll learn you're very significant
yes, you're an important speck of sand,
You're more than just some tiny particle
on this massive chunk of land
Now that you have Jesus on your team
hold on tightly to His hand
He'll show you the mighty things He can do
with just a tiny speck of sand.

Ask Yourself

Why is it people rush around to do their daily stuff,
No matter what they seem to have it never is enough.
Big houses, big cars, and a bank account that's fat,
They never get around to this for they're always doing that.
Rushing children out the door going ever which a way,
To busy doing other stuff to watch them while they play.
Exactly what is it these people hope to find,
Missing life's simple pleasures going thru this daily grind?
Is a bigger house better or a better car "the bomb",
Or is it more worth your while to be your children's mom?
When the years vanish and you retire,
will it matter what you had,
Or will your family remember you took time to be their dad?
I know we all need money to survive life on earth,
But is money what we really need to discover life's true worth?
I think you know my answer but to each his own be true,
I'll leave it up to you, my friend, to decide what's right for you.

Blind Ambition

If I'm not real careful, I could completely miss the boat.
For as I do my daily things, I often tend to gloat.
Thinking the things I get done are accomplished just by me,
I take the credit from my God, and fully fail to see.
Long before I took a breath and God brought me to earth,
Was He who planned these daily things and gave my life worth.
He's the one who knows my thoughts, and gives me what I need,
Even when I'm plain selfish, and my actions show my greed.
Because I'm God's handiwork, He knows where I am weak,
He sets a good example for me, and turns the other cheek.
He shows me how I should forgive, and blesses me each day,
Through the awesome love He's shown,
I've learned He is the way.
Not only does God hold the key, with His one and only Son,
I realize things I thought I did, are really what God has done.

Boundaries

No doubt boundaries set the tone
for how you live your life,
How you treat your fellow man
your children and your wife.
If you want to have a healthy life
boundaries are a great place to start,
For a life with no boundaries, my friend,
will soon fall apart.
You're just a simple human being
and your human traits will win,
Without proper boundaries, my friend,
you'll live a life filled with sin.
I've heard it said the sky's the limit
and I suppose that sayings true,
But, even blue sky's turn dark and gray
if there's no limit to what you do.
It's not a good idea to be undisciplined
and put your boundaries upon a shelf,
Remember your life will have no boundaries
unless you put them there yourself.
You can do without having boundaries,
the choice is up to you,
But, I've warned you about the pitfalls
so, you can't claim you never knew.
So, set some boundaries and set the tone
for how you'll live your life,
How you'll treat your fellow man
your children and your wife.
You will find you're much happier

when your world's not falling apart,
You'll realize if the sky's your limit
boundaries are the place you must start.

Color Blind

First, God created Heaven and Earth, and then He created us,
So, how can the difference we have create such a fuss.
We fail to see the judgment we pass, is fully soaked with sin,
When we judge God's creation by just the color of their skin.
Deep inside we have a flaw, did God create that too?
No, it's certainly not a trait from Christ when I belittle you.
I feel God looks at us and it fills His heart with shame,
For outside the color of our skin, He made us all the same.
How pleased do I think God would be, were He to look and find
each child He made, loved the next, like He was color blind.
What must we do to change this trend,
and make a brand-new start,
Where men of every race are judged
by the content of their heart.
I could be wrong, I'm not sure if this change can ever take place,
For its universal and not just one, that judge the other race.
Though we all live and share the rights, in a country that is free,
We separate ourselves by race, and somehow fail to see.
The color of the skin of man doesn't really show,
The things by God's design about man, we really need to know.
No matter how unfair it seems your fellow man has been,
God never intended for us to judge each other,
by the color of our skin.

Daily Choice

Another day has come and gone
and here I am again,
Grateful, blessed, and still alive
with Jesus as my friend.
Some days it goes unnoticed
as I slip into my day,
I seem ungrateful for my blessings,
and I don't take time to pray.
I should start my day with prayer
yet I rush right out the door,
God is still faithful to bless me
like He's always done before.
I still feel His mighty presence
as the wind whispers through the trees,
I'm reminded of His endless love,
and it brings me to my knees.
For a moment while on my knees
I hear His still small voice,
I realize to stay close to God
I must make a daily choice.
I know no one will protect me
and love me like God can,
I know when I trust and lean on Him
I'm a completely different man.
I must somehow figure out
how to make this daily choice,
How to say my prayers each morning,
and how to listen to God's voice.
Yes, on my knees is where I belong

I need this daily choice intact,
For there'd be no blessings of a new day
without the Lord, and that's a fact.
So, here I am once again, Lord
I'm begging with you please,
Help me be thankful for each new day,
and help me start it on my knees.

Daily Recipe

There's a simple plan to follow
to enjoy abundant life today,
Don't let past problems or future worries
produce thoughts that impede your way.
I'm only passing along information
God's Word clearly states,
Although I'm not sure I have a case
that these are things God truly hates.
He does however strongly suggest
today is where our focus should be,
And obeying the truths of His word,
always comes with a guarantee.
That's right, my friend, a guarantee
known as a promise from God,
If you know the same God I know
you're not likely to think that's odd.
First, God says cast your cares on Him
then ask Him for His help,
He tells us to leave it all with Him
for that's the most important step.
Then we're free to live life today,
and enjoy the peace God brings,
The final step to seal the deal
is to meditate on all good things.
In case somehow you missed it, my friend,
go back and read the last eight lines,
God always reveals His truths and promises,
And He always gives clear signs.
As you will see God clearly states

to have calm in your storm today,
Cast, ask, leave, and meditate
with your problems when you pray.
Then past problems, and future worries
won't fill your today with strife,
You'll be free to claim God's promise,
and go live today's abundant life.

Dealing with Death

It's hard to lose people you love
yet it happens along life's way,
We know if we keep on living
it's the price life makes us pay.
No one can escape this road
it is traveled by us all
The question is how will you live
until you receive your call.
As long as you see a new sunrise,
and your given another day,
Losing your friends and loved ones
will always come into play.
How do we travel this lonely road
and keep our hearts intact,
You may not agree with me,
but to me it's a cold hard fact.
As you travel this great big world,
and you lose special people you love,
It's important to learn if they know Jesus,
and have a home in heaven above.
Don't get it wrong, you'll still feel pain
death always takes its toll,
But you'll rest a little easier, my friend,
when you know Jesus has their soul.
It's a win-win situation for sure
if you have this story to tell,
For they'll be with Jesus in heaven forever,
and their soul will be saved from hell.
One day death will come calling for you,

and it'll be your time to go,
But at least you'll be headed to heaven
to see people you love and know.
As long as the sun keeps rising
and you keep walking down life's road,
Share Jesus with the people you love
because it'll sure help lighten your load.
The way to live until it's your time
is sharing Jesus with everyone you see,
Friends and family, no matter their problems
you know it's Jesus who holds the key.
Now you may get a little lonely
but your heart will be intact,
If you remember Jesus is the answer,
and friend, that's a cold hard fact.
One day you'll share eternity in heaven
with all your family and friends,
You can make up for the time you lost
for your home in heaven never ends.

Decide For Yourself

What if God sent you a greeting card, telling you when life
would end,
Would you keep it to yourself, or share it with your friends?
It's worth contemplating what we'd do, if we knew just
when we'd die,
But instead, we take for granted and our lives pass us by.
I'd like to know, I don't think it would cause me stress,
In fact, I'd write a thank you note, and send it to God's address.
I'd let God know I appreciate the heads up note He
decided to send,
Then I'd share the news with everyone I considered to be
my friend.
I'd tell my friends and family my fate, I'd like them to know,
Sharing I believe would create bonds that flourish and grow.
All too often we treat our lives as though we'll never die,
We leave friends and family behind to grieve and wonder why.
That's my thoughts, how about you, would you share your
greeting card,
Or, would you keep it to yourself because sharing bad
news is hard?
No matter which choice you'd make, remember this
important fact,
The days you spend unwisely now, you can never get them back.
So, friend, don't you think, you should share with family
and friends,
The things you keep putting off, before your life on earth
really ends.

Give or Take

What really is important in this life I now live,
Should I place focus on myself or to others should I give?
Now at first it seems so easy, after all is it not true,
In most things that are done each day, I don't consider you.
In days gone by I've seen myself choose a selfish way to be,
But the example of Christ on the cross has helped me to see.
To give of me to someone else comes from deep inside
The love of God in my heart, I should never choose to hide.
It's easier said than done, and this challenge I face each day
The tools I feel I lack, I'll ask for when I pray.
I'm sure to always struggle in this "fleshly" life I live,
Still, I'll remember God's great gift, and to others I shall give.
For God's great gift on Calvary has made my heart believe,
It's more blessed to give, my friend, than it is when you receive.

I Wonder Why

We know God made man and woman all those years ago,
I'm not questioning God, but there's some things I'd
like to know.
If companionship was His intent for Adam and Eve as mates,
How come He made them so different instead of giving more
common traits?
I wonder why women like soft and cuddly, and love a big
bouquet of flowers,
While a man likes rough and rugged and loves to sit and fish
for hours.
I wonder why women are so emotional, and so beautiful to
man's eye,
While men were made so logical and feel they're weak if they
should cry.
I wonder why a woman desires friendship, before intimacy can
take place,
While a man wants to make "good love" every time he
sees her face.
I wonder why women like shopping malls, and gossiping when
they're together,
While men want to drink their beer and hunt, regardless of
the weather.
I wonder why status and power, are so important to identify
man's life,
While love in the home and security, are important to his wife.
Even at an early age, we see this difference in girls and boys,
It's easy to see how different they are, by the way they choose
their toys.
I wonder why boys like balls and trucks, and playing in the dirt,

While girls like Barbie dolls, and wearing makeup and a skirt.
In the spirit of understanding, why we're as different as
night and day,
I'll admit it keeps life interesting, as we struggle to get our way.
You may think you have good answers to these questions I
have posed,
Yet, the truth of the matter, my friend, is it's God who
really knows.
I'll try to understand our differences, as the days and
years go by,
Even though I'm sure God knows best, I'll always wonder why.

In Return

There are times I stop in total awe,
from the fullness of a day.
To praise the Lord my God above,
and let Him hear me pray.
He pours His blessings down on me,
in each and every way,
To stop and voice my thanks to Him,
is the least that I should say.
Each day I rise is a gift, you see,
for the Lord loves me still.
He urges me each day I rise,
to seek and do His will.
With purpose He has made me,
for this purpose I still live.
The blessings He pours down on me,
to others I should give.
Each day I rise, I'll share the grace
My Lord has given me.
I'll share my faith with others,
so they too can be free.
For Christ is the answer,
on that I'm really clear.
And to share my faith with others,
is the reason I'm still here.

Life's Problems

I think it'd be cool to have all the answers
to the problems in life I face,
I'm sure if that were a reality
I'd live life at a different pace.
I wouldn't worry about this or that,
or how, or when and why,
I'd always have the perfect answer,
and I'd have it the very first try.
It's hard enough taking care of me
and the problems that life presents,
It seems having all the answers to life
still doesn't make good sense.
Every plan has a few flaws
looking closer this seems to hold true,
Maybe I'd have all life's answers,
but you'll be wanting them too.
Sure, I'll have all the answers I need
that's not the problem I face
I'll be busy giving everyone answers,
and right back in the ole rat race.
If that's the way it's going to be
when I have all the answers to life,
I'd rather search for the answers
that solve problems for me and my wife.
I'm not ready to solve the world's problems,
and hand out answers all day,
There's a chance people wouldn't believe me,
or even listen to a word I say.
This is really no different, my friend,

than any other problem we solve,
We have a hundred different answers,
but they always seem to dissolve.
Soon we realize life has its problems,
and there's no answer, that's just a fact.
No matter how smart we think we are
sometimes the deck's just stacked.
So, settle in and accept it, my friend,
and try to enjoy your life,
I think we've made a mighty good case,
it will only cause you more strife.
We all have problems, so solve your own,
you'll avoid a much bigger scar.
Having the answers to all life's problems
makes them bigger than they already are.

Live to Give

As I have grown older, and the years pass me by,
I thought I'd understand, but I still question why.
In a land that's as great as where I now live,
Why do so many take, and so few people give?
I may be naïve in the way I think,
But, I've seen when you take, what you have starts to shrink.
To get richer you must give, although that sounds absurd,
That's clearly what you'll see if you closely read God's Word.
It's the example of our Lord, He showed us long ago,
When we become givers, His blessing really flow.
We crave money and things, we brag and we boast,
We have forgotten what God says matters most.
I'm not saying it's wrong to live a good life,
But, its money and things that bring about our strife.
Our focus should be on the life still ahead,
Where money and things won't matter when we're dead.
When up in heaven, God will supply our every need,
Money won't exist, and there won't be any greed.
Can't we get the big picture, while we're here on earth,
It's giving and not taking, that gives our life true worth.
Maybe I'm not naïve, for what I believe sure seems true,
So, test me if you'd like, and see if I won't give to you.
I have gotten older, and I still may question why,
But, a chance to give to others, I won't let that pass me by.

Not Today Satan

To him I probably look feeble
and too weak to hold my own,
But, I warned him it won't be easy
I'm not fighting my battles alone.
I see him lurking in the shadows
he's in the darkness waitin,
These days I'm leaning on the Lord
and I'm not losing to ole satan.
He's cunning and he's sly,
he tries to lure my heart away.
He don't want me close to God
to hear what He might have to say.
I've started to learn his tactics
I see all the traps he's baitin,
I make sure to stay close to God
so I don't fall prey to ole satan.
satan would constantly defeat me
if God wasn't on my side,
There's not a trick known to man
ole satan hasn't tried.
satan may think I'm weak
and too feeble to hold my own,
But, he don't realize I'm in my Bible
and my knowledge of God has grown.
I keep learning God's truths and promises
that's why satan keeps on hatin,
In days gone by he'd beat me up
but now I'm beating up on satan.
I'm no longer drinking milk,

I'm living on the meat of the Word.
I make sure I let satan know
just in case he hasn't heard.
I'm no longer weak and feeble,
these days I don't feel near as prone
I don't think so, not today satan,
for I'm not fighting my battles alone.

Rainbow Legend

The colors of the rainbow
so pretty to the eyes.
God's promise to His people
stretched across the skies.
I'm sure you've heard the legend
many times before, my friend,
How you'll find a pot of gold
if you're at the rainbows end.
We're always trying to alter
the things God puts in place,
But there is no pot of gold
I'm quite certain that is the case.
Although there is no pot of gold
it's meaning has far more worth,
It's a symbol of God's promise
to never again flood the earth.
I think everyone would agree
the rainbow's a sight to behold,
Still, I hate to spoil the legend,
my friend, there is no pot of gold.
There's just the colors of the rainbow
from orange to green and red,
They appear after a rainfall
to remind us what God said.
It's painted in magnificent fashion
in colors bright and bold,
It's all about God's promise, my friend,
it's not about a pot of gold.

Repeat Offender

You've been down this road before
it's a familiar path you trod,
You know you'll never give it up
until you give it to God.
Time and time again, you see,
you can't do it on your own,
For some reason you leave God out
and try to fight your battle alone.
You know the problem, you know the answer
You know them both quite well,
But, the chains of habit grip you tight
and once again cause you to fail.
How many times must you fall victim
to the same sinful routine,
Before you'll give it all to God
so He can change your scene.
The answer is simple, the problem's not
I know your problem is real,
Trust me friend, I've walked in your shoes
I know how it makes you feel.
You want change and you need relief
still you do the same thing again,
You're nothing more than a repeat offender
gripped by the chains of unwanted sin.
You keep making the same mistakes
you feel you'll never break free,
The answer is to give your heart to Jesus
for Jesus holds the key.
You have a choice, you have free will

you can choose to feel vulnerable and prone,
Or you can give your problem to Jesus
so you're not fighting your battle alone.
I was once that repeat offender
I didn't like the situation I was in,
I kept making the same bad choices
I was shackled by the chains of sin.
Then I decided to call on Jesus
and He set this captive free,
Friend, call on Jesus, He'll do for you
the same thing He did for me.
My God is a real chain breaker
although there's still a part you must play,
But, you won't be fighting your battle alone
you'll have Jesus beside you every day.

Rewind and Realize

If we had a time machine for the people who have doubt,
and we could go back to the beginning, and see how God
brought things about.
How many people would crawl inside, and return to that very
first day,
And how many would stay and believe The Theory of
Evolution way.
I pose this question because it seems like people play
dumb and deaf,
They wouldn't believe God's handy-work if they saw it
for themself.
It's a complex world I will admit, but if we were to take a poll,
The results would show, many people still doubt who's
in control.
It's sad to think there are people who don't rely on God for help,
For by His strength I live each day, and He knows my every step.
Still, many believe there is no God, and the world
somehow evolved,
They rely upon themselves alone, for life's problems to
be solved.
Since there is no time machine to carry us back to that very
first day,
There will always be doubters who believe The Theory of
Evolution way.
But friend, Jesus died upon the cross so eternal life could
be received,
And it's there for all who change their belief from a theory man
conceived.

Show Me the Money

If you had lots of money, I mean more than you could spend,
Is there any doubt everyone you see would consider you
their friend.
Would it really be worth your while, to have a pocket
full of dough,
Dealing with folks who call you friend, even people you
don't know.
Now I am not suggesting, having money would be all bad,
It's just the things people do for it, is really kinda sad.
All of us have some of it, and some more than they need,
And yes it's true not everyone is consumed by selfish greed.
Yet time and time again I see, where money is involved,
Problems get created, instead of problems being solved.
"All is fair in love and war" and with money so it seems,
Far too often we lose friends, trying to fulfill our own dreams.
Funny how a bunch of cash can make you lose your grip,
Somehow a need for getting things can cloud a good friendship.
I'd like to think if I were rich, these things wouldn't
happen to me,
Sometimes I wish I'd have the chance, just so I could see.
How about you, would money change the important things in
your life?
Would you allow the money trap to fill your days with strife?
Could you deal with all the folks, who want a "piece of your pie"?
I'll bet you're no different than me, you'd like the chance to try.

Stance over Circumstance

Everyday your circumstances
are different than before,
There's no way to ever know
just what might be in store.
Things happen so fast at times
it can put you in a trance,
But if you're going to live for God
you've got to learn to take a stance.
To take a stand and follow Christ
is a test that can be stern,
But don't change with your circumstance
every time life takes a turn.
You've got to choose your stance
and don't let life beat you down,
Each time your circumstances change
be determined to stand your ground.
It may not seem that important
if you look at just a glance,
But the devil is always lurking
and looking for his chance.
He'll try to pull you away from God
and make you dance his dance,
Don't give in stand strong in Christ
choose stance over circumstance.
It's a simple little thought, my friend,
yet it's words ring mighty true,
Choose stance over circumstance
so the devil don't get the best of you.

The Cost of Living

Exactly what is this thing we call the "American Dream",
Let's review the facts, and soon you'll see exactly what I mean.
Everything but salaries are up and going thru the roof,
If you need further evidence, view your paycheck as the proof.
Try to have more children, they'll break you before their birth,
Try to sell your house, and it's no longer what it's worth.
Try to fill your car with gas, look how the price just rose,
Try to educate your kids, and you'll pay right through the nose.
Try to keep your family warm during winter when it's cold,
Try and care for mom and dad, now that they are getting old.
Try and replace the family car,
and buy the cheapest one on the lot,
For the average American man, it takes almost all he's got.
Try and see the doctor, to keep your family in good health,
Just to get good insurance these days, takes a world of wealth.
No longer can we get good deals on things we think are groovy,
Heck, now it cost an arm and leg just to go and see a movie.
I guess the vacation I take each year is the thing I'll have to axe,
You understand there's nothing left
after Uncle Sam takes his tax.
With each passing year we live, inflation will probably grow,
And it's true, things aren't as cheap as they were years ago.
Despite the fact things cost more, and there's little left to save,
Never forget this is the land of the free, and home to all to brave.

True Worth

As I wander thru this wilderness
on this place we all call earth,
I think about the life I've lived
and I contemplate it's worth.
I know I've done a thing or two
to please the God I trust,
Still, there's more I need to do
before this body returns to dust.
Of all the things I feel I've learned
as I've lived my earthly life,
The most important is trusting God
to deal with all my toil and strife.
The blood of Jesus gives me worth,
and seals my heavenly fate,
It's what gives me the peace I have,
and makes life on earth so great.
Still, the thing I contemplate
is did a Godly life I live
Did I share the love of Jesus,
and did I strive to always give.
Certainly Jesus knows my worth,
and He'll share with me on high,
But, the proper time to show my worth
is before I meet Him in the sky.
So, as I contemplate my worth
to figure out just what I've done,
I realize the important of trusting God
and telling others about His Son.
If I can walk hand-in-hand with God

and share Jesus while here on earth,
Then I think it's safe to say, my friend,
I've lived a life that's had true worth.

Unfinished Business

If my life were almost over, I mean really near the end,
Are there any paths I'd need to cross, any fences I should mend?
As I ponder on this question one thing I know is true,
This is not my final resting place; I'm only passing thru.
Once I have departed and left everything behind,
What is it I will have left for other folks to find?
Sure there'll be stuff like cars and homes
and money that I saved,
Yet the thing of worth I'll leave behind is
the influence that I gave.
There are paths I must cross and fences yet to mend,
But I'll need the help of Christ my Lord to leave a proper trend.
I don't know when my life's over or if the end is really near,
I only know God left His Word and made it very clear.
With a purpose I was made from the first day of my birth,
I'll leave behind an influence, what will mine be worth?

What If

What if we could have our way, no matter what the cost?
What if we lived our life each day, and no time were ever lost?
What if each time we broke our bank, our account only grew?
What if we never went to work, and no one ever knew?
What if no hunger pains would come, even if we never ate?
What if our lives were filled with love because we never
learned to hate?
What if each time we helped someone our days were full
of strife?
What if when we act selfishly, it cost days off our life?
What if every time we took in air, we could never catch
our breath?
What if we never had a life because no one conquered death?
What if God made Adam and Eve before He made Heaven
and Earth?
What if satan were allowed to decide what your soul is
really worth?
Though these may not be your what if's, you're sure to
have your own,
For when it comes to questioning life, I'm certainly not alone.
It's true, my friend, as we live life, things sometimes
do seem odd,
Yet, I am certain it could be worse, what if there were no God?
But, we have a Father, His Son, and the gift of the Holy Ghost,
Accepting God's gift is the "What if" question that really
matters most.

Ask yourself life's "What if's" but remember this
important thing,
They all mean nothing without the joy, this gift from God
can bring.

What's the Difference

What makes a man be selfish
while another lives life to share,
How can one reach out to others
while the next don't seem to care.
You only have two choices
one seems bad and one seems good,
Still, we often struggle to give
even when we know we should.
Giving isn't always easy
we've all been in those shoes,
Knowing who we really are inside
is determined by what we choose.
Yet, holding on is a natural thing
when push comes to shove,
That's probably what we all will do
without help from God above.
The difference between the selfish man
and the one who lives to share,
Is something deep inside his heart
that seems to make him care.
It is God who changes the heart of man
and shows him how to live,
It's the love of God inside the man
that makes him want to give.

Whatever Happened

Whatever happened to balls and jacks and Tonka toy trucks,
Trying to catch a greasy pig and raising baby ducks.
Swimming at the lake all day and catching lightning
bugs by night,
When children met outside and they played with all their might.
We didn't have a bunch of things, but the simple life was grand,
We entertained ourselves all day with a big box full of sand.
What happened to baseball in the yard and enjoying a
sunny day,
Now kids stay inside and it's video games they play.
I'll be the first to freely admit technology has opened up doors,
But we've gotten so out of balance, we don't teach kids
their chores.
Give them whatever they want and let them have their way,
We don't demand respect or manners, nor teach them to obey.
Whatever happened to taking away privileges or "Boy, go
get my belt,"
Punishment that did some good because it really could be felt.
These days we make a threat or give a little five minute timeout.
Even that is usually done wrong, where it only causes doubt.
Whatever happened to those times we called "the good
ole days,"
Although we're now blessed with much, those days deserve
our praise.
Whatever happened to the "good ole days" and the way we
used to live,
A slower pace and a family life, for that what I wouldn't give.

Who's Your God

An amazing nation always has been
built on "In God We Trust",
A burning desire for what those words are on
has caused our nation to rust.
It's not just the money, but our love for it
that's caused our nation's decay,
The trust in the guidebook God gave us,
gets pushed farther and farther away.
Over time we've seen many good changes,
yet it's a beaten down path we trod,
There are many believers, but even they
choose to make money their god
Was there hidden meaning in 30 pieces of silver
that caused Judas to sell his soul?
We didn't grasp, but now we clearly see
today, money still plays the same role.
The beliefs and freedoms that were in place
as a nation we now push aside,
Should inspire Christian people to make a stand
and not just proclaim they tried.
We may not be Judas and it may not be silver,
but still we're like bees craving honey.
Look how we sin over and over again,
so we can obtain more money.
Try as we may, we can never deny
satan uses money in our lives to disrupt,
Though there are many good people with pure hearts,
as a nation we still are corrupt.

Why Regret

Why regret what we can't change
from days now passed us by,
It does no good to live our past
and continue to wonder why.
Our focus should be on here and now
and keeping today on track,
No matter how much we regret our past
we can never get it back.
There are things we'd all re-do
with information we now know,
But God tells us to live today
and use regrets to learn and grow.
Don't forget while simple, my friend,
it still holds mighty true,
God has a purpose for everything
that happens to me and you.
Don't ask why and regret your past
just leave it all behind,
Instead, ask God as you learn and grow
what He desires for you to find.
Simply changing your why to what
will change the results you get,
By asking what, you'll seek God's purpose
and you won't focus on your regret.

Section Two

ALL IN THE FAMILY

For Reflection:

Everyone understands the importance of family. We should always take time to love and appreciate them.

A new commandment I give unto you, That ye love one another; as I have loved you, that ye also love one another.

—John 13:34

All in the Family

A Dad's Love

Hardly a day goes by in my life,
I don't see this special space.
It can only be filled by the love of a Dad,
for no one can take his place.
I've heard it said and I'm sure it's true,
good Dads are a dying breed.
Still, a child doesn't know and continues to look,
for a Dad to fulfill their needs.
Though sad it's true in the world today,
Mom's and Dad's fall apart.
The need of the child for the love of Dad,
is still in the little one's heart.
Often we see when a family fails,
a Father will go his own way.
To the child if the Father's a Dad,
there's still a big part He must play.
Life has changed, and the child may not have,
all the things that they once had,
They still have a need and no one can replace,
the special love of their Dad.
A Dad has the love a child desperately needs,
and nothing should keep them apart.
In the child's mind you still are their Dad,
and they seek your love in their heart.
If you're a Father who has gone his own way,
then you're not in your rightful place.
Remember your child still needs a Dad,
so return to your special space.

A Double Life

I have a mother and a father
we always stay in touch,
I have an older and younger brother
and I love them very much.
They are my temporary family
and we share a special bond,
They are very special people to me
and my memories of them are fond.
I value and cherish these people
and the times we have together,
There's no doubt I can count on them
when I face life's stormy weather.
The love my heart holds for them
and the love they've given back,
Has certainly been a key
to help keep my life on track.
Yet, this is not my only family
and to you that may seem odd,
But it's true I have a forever family,
it's called the family of God.
I have a Heavenly Father
who loves me as His own,
He loved me before my birth
and now that I am grown.
He loves me more than my earthly family
I don't understand how or why,
Still, I know I'm in His forever family
and I'll reign with Him on high.
My earthly family is part

of God's forever family, too,
We strive to include our Heavenly father
in whatever we choose to do.
We understand the storms of life
is where satan will choose to lurk,
When we trust in our forever family,
that's when God does His best work.
So, it's true I have two families
one temporary and one forever,
I need the love I get from both
to withstand the storms I endeavor.
Join God's forever family, my friend,
and you can live a life like mine,
Although you may live a double life
it'll be by God's design.
We all have a temporary family
that's something we all understand,
Yet, God created His forever family
and you're part of God's master plan.

A Perfect Pair

Mom and dad a perfect pair
from God sent long ago,
They've stood the test of time and trials
to watch their children grow.
Now three boys wasn't always easy
and at times it was no fun,
But somehow the perfect pair survived,
and the two are still as one.
Not just any dad or mom I say,
that hardly is the case,
But a perfect pair from God above
sent to a special place.
A place where boys would need the love
a perfect pair could give,
A place to show them how a Heavenly Father
would like for them to live.
Of all the many lessons, this perfect pair revealed,
Was the love of God our Father they perfectly instilled.
The perfect pair worked mighty hard
on this gift sent from above,
They showed three boys how they should live,
and taught them how to love.
These same boys now are men,
and have families of their own,
The perfect pair from God above,
sees seeds that once were sown.
I hope these boys have made them proud,
but even better still
I'm glad this perfect pair from God

was seeking out His will.
Though much of life is yet to live,
I'd really like to share,
I thank God for the perfect pair,
who never failed to show they care.

Thanks Mom and Dad for honoring God,
staying together, and being the perfect pair.

A Special Son

Seems like yesterday when you were born,
but its' now twelve years ago.
Many good memories have come and gone,
as I've watched you learn and grow.
From the very first time I laid eyes on you,
I knew you were a special son.
I never imagined the joy you'd bring,
and that you'd be so much fun.
It's true that dads and sons do bond
in a very special way.
But, often times your dad forgot
to share things He should say.
I know there are times I embarrass you,
not being "cool", or talking too loud,
Other times I simply forget to say,
Son, you sure make me proud.
Many days I've watched you son,
you're talented, yes, it's true.
Still, I forgot to say thanks,
for the many things you do.
I know you know I love you,
but in case you've wondered why,
These words I write so you will know
with each day that passes by.
Your dad is so proud of you,
and He thinks you're number one,
God could have never given to me
a more incredible, special son.

Love, Dad

Is It True

Is it true I must share my words, to ensure you will know,
Or will you learn from me by the actions that I show.
Is it true the traits I watch in you, I can clearly see,
are the result of all the times, you were clearly watching me.
It's true those little eyes, watch me so they can learn,
I must always be aware, though the test can be quite stern.
Is it true as you grow, I should view this as a chore,
or will it be a privilege my son, as I learn to love you more.
Is it true as time goes on, I'll feel I've done my best,
Or will I feel my efforts have failed this rugged test.
It's true I must give my all, to raise my son today,
Not only by my actions, but with words I choose to say.
Is it true the actions I choose, will be good for you to see,
So, when you're grown and gone, I'll be proud you're
just like me.
Is it true all the things I say, will help you understand,
All I teach you now my son, will help you become a man.
Its true actions and words, will both play a big part,
I'll never forget - what you hear and see molds your
precious heart.

Life's Little Blessings

Is there anything more precious, you'll experience in this life,
Than the gift of having children, as a husband and a wife.
There's nothing to compare it to, the joy having children brings,
They'll test and try your patience, while tugging your
heart strings.
Try to teach them right from wrong, so they're prepared for all
life's tests,
Good parents, when a child is grown, wants to feel they've done
their best.
The things we teach may differ, and to others may seem odd,
Remember it's important to teach that they always trust in God.
There will be many times, we fail our children along the way,
Yet we never go wrong, my friend, when we teach them
how to pray.
Raising children is a blessing, God gave to each of us,
Even though they make us mad, and we sometimes want to cuss.
As we face the challenge of children, remember the
results we get,
Come from what we instill in them, and the examples
that we set.
Relish the joys your children bring, but remember to do
your part,
Teach them every last thing you know and put Jesus in
their heart.

My Pride and Joy

I have a son named Austin, he's the best kid on earth,
It's hard to put into words what I believe he's really worth.
He's my pride and joy, and I'll admit he is a lot of fun,
If I could choose from all children, I'd choose Austin to
be my son.
When he was still a young boy, just one or two years old,
It became apparent my pride and joy, had a heart as
pure as gold.
He's a talented kid and smart too, he's wise beyond his years,
he's bold and brave with confidence, it seems there's
nothing he fears.
Not a perfect kid, for no kids are, that's why God gave
him to me,
I just hope I can raise him, to be all he can be.
Being a dad to Austin, I'll admit has been a test,
Still, to have such an awesome son, I truly do feel blessed.
So far so good, twelve years gone by, it's been a furious pace,
I'm convinced my pride and joy, is too precious to replace.
It's hard to explain what he's really worth, God's priceless
work of art,
This I know, he's my pride and joy that I love with all my heart.

Parental Guidance

What is it in the children's heart, that impel them to defy,
No matter what advice we give, they always question why.
It seems throwing up our hands, would be a better way to go,
but our judgment reveals, they'll need help if they're to grow.
It usually takes time, for a child to earn their role,
and understand by God's design, that a parent be in control.
Children always push the lines, we must pass their daily test,
It takes love and consistency, to help them thrive and do
their best.
Is it not true that years ago, we played our children's part,
We drove our own parent's nuts, with the defiance of our heart.
From our past we understand, what a difference a good
parent makes,
So, we can raise our children right, for we now know
what it takes.
We see as we raise our children, they think they're so smart,
It takes them years to realize their best interest was in our heart.
As a parent we must recognize, as children they're not mature,
The daily test they present is a challenge we must endure.
For now, show them patience, and answer their questions why,
Teach them right from wrong and mold their hearts to not defy.
We'll blink our eyes and they'll be gone, and have children of
their own,
The things they teach their children will come from seeds we
have sown.

Stay the Course

There is a time as a child grows up, they think they know it all,
lessons are learned the hard way, when they run before
they crawl.
A natural progression, it must occur, as the child comes into
their own,
they skin their knees and bloody their nose, making decisions
like they're grown.
It's hard to understand why children think, they know the right
paths to choose,
they won't listen to mom and dad, who've walked many miles in
their shoes.
Children think they know it all, but as a parent you must persist,
teach your child what they need, though you know they'll resist.
It may seem it does no good, and the child has not learned,
Stay the course and with time, their respect you will
have earned.
It won't change that they know it all, certainly much
more than you,
Just know one day they'll understand, the things you put
them thru.
When your child is grown and has children, they'll look back on
time and see,
They thought they knew it all, but mom and dad knew
more than me.
They will have smart children, who now know more than they,

They'll hear themselves saying things, years ago they
heard you say.
Just stay the course and know one day, although they know
more than you,
They'll love you and understand, you helped make their dreams
come true.

The Family of God

The Family of God is a special place
you'll find folks of every kind,
There's one thing they all have in common
they have Jesus on their mind.
People are people so they aren't perfect
yet they are usually in one accord,
They meet at church several times each week
and together they worship the Lord.
There's laughing and crying, praising and prayer
as the Family of God convenes,
Some family members wear a suit and tie
while others wear a t-shirt and jeans.
Most folks don't mind, they understand
It's not about the clothes you wear,
It's all about loving the Lord
and showing other folks you care.
Come join the Family of God, my friend,
you'll find our arms open wide,
We're not perfect, like I said we're people,
we all have something to hide.
It's understood when we come together
regardless of where you've been,
You are loved by the Heavenly Father
it is He who forgives your sin.
Don't let your sins keep you away
for to God you are a winner,
After all, church is where you belong,
it's a hospital for the sinner.
We'll bandage you up and give you a crutch

then help you lean on the Lord,
We'll sing praises and worship God
in our family you'll never be bored.
The Family of God is a special place
I'm sure you'll fit right in,
Once you've been around God's people
you'll want to come back again.
We'll celebrate Jesus and we'll pray together
no matter what paths you have trod,
Come on down to the church, my friend,
you're always welcome in the Family of God

Who'll Miss Me

It wouldn't surprise me, when my life is said and done,
If the person who misses me most, is my special only son.
There'll be other people I'm sure to meet, as I make my way
thru life,
Like the lady who is always there for me, I proudly call my wife.
There'll be teachers who spend countless hours to help my
child learn,
And lots of friends I'll get to know, whose respect I try to earn.
There'll be family members like Mom and Dad, who teach me all
they know,
Pastors and Sunday school teachers alike, who help me
spiritually grow.
There'll be doctors and nurses who tend to me, and help
when I'm sick,
Then there's those I'll barely know who judge me way to quick.
There'll be aunts and uncles, and other kin I see once a year,
My brothers and all their children, my heart has held so dear.
There'll be guys I work with, who'll see me every day,
Teammates at the ball field that enjoy the games we play.
There are lots of other people I'll meet, who are there by
God's design,
I'm sure along the path of life, I'll meet almost every kind.
But, there's something about your own children, words
can't explain,
They bring life's greatest joys, and I'm sure they feel the same.
That's why when my life has ended, and there's no more
time for fun,
The person who's sure to miss me most, is my special only son.

Section Three

DEAL WITH IT

For Reflection:

You have your own story, with challenges that are unique. Still, there are some things in life we all must deal with.

I can do all things through Christ which strengtheneth me.
                              —Philippians 4:13

Deal With It

Faith

How can I place trust in a God I can't really see?
Should I believe from millions of people, He chooses to love me?
When I experience the unexplained, do I credit God with these?
Do I follow folks I see in church, who have fallen to their knees?
If God made me and placed a void that only He can fill,
How is it I have fleshly traits that go against His will?
Can I be sure there is a God, who brought everything about?
What is it that I really need, to rid me of my doubt?
Must I face there are things, I may never know,
And trust a God I can't see, so my faith in him can grow?
In His word, God made it clear, by faith I must believe,
It's by faith, not by sight, His blessings I'll receive.
Seeing is believing, but faith is just God's way,
To teach me to trust in Him, as I face another day.
Now when I question how or when, or wonder what to do,
God reminds me to have faith, so I can share His love with you.

Fear

The biggest fear is in your head
that's just the way it goes,
The more you fear fear itself
the more you'll find it grows.
Fear is a hurdle we all must face
Yes, it's a valid foe,
Unless you figure it out, my friend,
there's no peaceful place to go.
Fear will take you to your knees
and crush the bravest soul,
The battle you fight within yourself
no doubt will take its toll.
There's only one way to win this battle
that we all possess within,
It's to admit that fear really exist
then your victory can begin.
You'll never conquer fear, my friend,
unless you admit that you're afraid,
For its fear who holds the cards
and knows how this game is played.
Fear would have you just deny
there's a fear that you must face,
So you won't even challenge fear
and fear can keep you in your place.
You know you've heard it many times
so don't play dumb and deaf,
For there's really nothing to fear
it is only fear itself.
In case somehow from what you've heard

my point you may have missed,
It's to not deny that you have fears
but to admit they exist.
If you face your fears and don't deny
then victory is in your sight,
Still, remember fear's a valid foe
and won't give up without a fight.
Follow these tips and a simple truth
that facing your fears will teach,
Then the victories you desire fighting fears
will be well within your reach.

Forgiveness

If there's one thing I really need, it's forgiveness I would say,
I find I'm less than perfect, as I go through each new day.
I often disappoint myself, and hurt the ones I love,
When others won't forgive me, I get forgiveness from above.
I often get forgiveness, and forgiveness I must give,
Unless we get and give forgiveness, life's too hard to live.
We all do wrong to others, and the results sure take a toll,
But something about forgiveness brings freedom to our soul.
Forgiveness was the example, set by Christ upon the cross,
When I choose to not forgive, it is I who suffers loss.
Next time I have hurt someone, or a wrong is done towards me
I'll remember forgiveness is the answer, and it's a gift to
share for free.

Greed

Though it's always been a problem,
it's more prevalent these days.
Even folks who once were honest
seem content to change their ways.
Right is right and wrong is wrong,
there is no in between,
Yet folks of every race and creed,
justify to get more green.
Just look almost anywhere
you'll see this trend take place,
Still, a loving God forgives,
and provides amazing grace.
It's everywhere you look these days,
this terrible thing called greed,
Making good folks sell their soul
for things they don't even need.
The more you get the more you want,
or so the saying goes,
Why our hearts are filled with greed,
only Jesus really knows.
It's really sad to see
how our hearts have gone astray,
Often times we ask for more
when we bow our heads to pray.
We're told money is the root of all evil,
but God's Word we still don't heed.
We're far too busy obtaining more,
to help satisfy our greed.
Who's to say if it's worse,

than it was back years ago,
It may be, or maybe not,
but one thing is true I know.
There's a piece of greed in each of us,
that will be there till we die.
We won't get rid of that fleshly trait,
no matter how hard we try.
Still, If we put our faith in God,
and realize He gives life it's worth,
Greed won't be what rules our hearts,
as we live life here on earth.

Guilt

The hands of time allow the start
of the erosion that takes place,
When decisions made from yesterday
become mistakes we just can't face.
Each of us have done things
that tear down what we've built,
It's never long before we must deal
with our self-inflicted guilt.
Funny how the mind works
when we feel we've done wrong,
We try to justify our acts,
but our guilt is far too strong.
There's a healthy way to deal with guilt,
yet it's a high price we must pay,
For guilt can drain our energy
trying to make it through the day.
Maybe we should turn to God
to deal with how we feel,
God knows guilt robs our joy
and the effects of it are real.
He sees inside and knows we have
good intentions in our heart,
If we ask, He'll forgive our wrongs,
and give life a brand-new start.
Still, we must accept the grace God gives,
And forgive our own self too,
Then remember mistakes from yesterday
need not affect what we now do.
Take my advice, and trust in God,

see the peace only He can give,
Don't allow guilt to erode the years
you have left to live

Manners

Saying please and saying thank you
yes sir and yes mam' too,
Back in the day these were common words
that everybody knew.
As a matter of fact it was mandatory
you learned to say these things,
For if you didn't, you'd feel the wrath
disrespecting your elder brings.
Now a lack of manners to others
would certainly cause great regret,
Because good manners was standard procedure
no matter who it was you met.
Manners are no longer taught at home
to me this seems quite clear,
These days a please or thank you sir
are words you rarely ever hear.
Parents are often too self-absorbed
out of mind and out of sight,
They leave it upon their children
to decide what's wrong or right.
Since manners no longer are taught at home
you see exactly what you'd expect,
When children are never taught any manners,
they also never learn respect.
Children soon become adults
and have children of their own,
But they are rude and have no manners,
even though they now are grown.
So who's to teach the little ones manners,

as each new generation comes around,
When parents who have respect and manners
are so much harder to be found.
It's sad but true as time ticked on
good manners it seems got lost,
And if your honest you'll have to admit
it's come at quite a cost.
Back in the day respect and manners
they both went hand in hand,
For those of you who remember those days,
it's time to make a stand.
Don't be too busy in your own selfish world
take time to plant the seed,
Stand up for respect and stand up for manners
for these are traits our children need.

Patience

Patience is a virtue for those
who possess this valued trait,
Most of us are in the group
of folks who just can't wait.
What we want, we want now
waiting's not in the cards,
It's too easy to get our way
and waiting is just plain hard.
Our children have seen
how impatient the world has grown,
Surely we don't think they'll change
once they are on their own.
We know things won't change
we figure they'll follow our lead,
We admit we spoiled them rotten
with things they don't need.
Parents should teach patience
and that things must be earned,
But, patience isn't taught anymore,
so patience is never learned.
Instant gratification is such
a common trait these days,
That people who exhibit patience at all
are worthy of our praise.
Patience is a virtue,
and if we don't possess this valued trait,
How can we teach our children, that
good things come to those who wait.

Perception

For many years I've understood perception is the key,
It's not what life presents; it's how I perceive things to be.
Some see the glass half empty, while half full is others view,
Both are technically right, but the perceptions up to you.
There are times life is hard, and things aren't so great,
The way I see the glass myself, can cause quite some debate.
Some believe getting up their hopes is a recipe for disaster,
While others believe it helps attain their goals much faster.
Sometimes it's hard to see, life's problems in a positive light,
But, manage to find the good, you've already won half the fight.
If you have positive thoughts, they're sure to come about,
Still, many people find the negative and exercise their doubt.
You may see a half empty glass, and believe your
perceptions are true
You won't listen to anyone else, and you won't change your view.
Like everything else in life, there's pros and cons for each,
As for me, I'll see half full, and believe the other half's
in my reach.

Pride

Pride comes before the fall
I'm quite certain this will occur,
I read it in God's Word one day,
and it caused my heart to stir.
I realize the pride I have,
won't send my soul to hell,
Yet, I shouldn't allow my foolish pride
to cause my heart to swell.
Many times I feel
I've kept my pride at bay,
Other times I failed the test,
and said things I shouldn't say.
God's Word teaches me
to swallow my foolish pride,
It's hard to always do what's right,
and keep my thoughts inside.
God made me and gave me pride,
So, there are times when it is good,
Somehow, I must find its place,
and only use it when I should.

Shattered Dreams

Life is filled with disappointments, at least that's the
way it seems,
As we pick up broken pieces, of our lost and shattered dreams.
All too often the purpose of life, seems very unclear,
We lose a job, lose a friend, or a loved one that is dear.
Each of us have pain and hurt, as something we must face,
Which of us will struggle through with dignity and grace.
As we wake up to a new sunrise, our hearts are full of hope,
Yet, the new day's bumps and bruises make it hard to cope.
Still, we dare to venture on, for with a will, there is a way,
After all, dreams are born right here in the USA.
There's one simple thing a dreamer should never overlook,
It's hard to keep the dream intact with no instruction book.
That's okay, there's one sure way life won't lose its steam,
Be sure you have Jesus as the leader of your team.
He'll be there to help you, face all life's extremes,
He'll take your broken pieces and mend your shattered dreams.

Temptation

It's nothing new to you or I, It's a natural part of life,
It started in the Garden when Adam gave into his wife.
Because of man's choice that day, and satan's imagination,
We now deal with a daily thing, we simply call temptation.
No one gets a by on this, no one can be exempt,
satan is early to rise each day, and he lives his life to tempt.
Each of us must deal with satan, it's a path we each must trod,
The only way to stay on course, is to learn to trust in God.
He is the way, the truth, the life, and on Him we must rely,
Beating temptation alone is too hard, the devil is way too sly.
It's the devil's job each day, to tempt you like the rest,
God allows the devil to put us through this daily test.
Temptation is a master plan, though to me it's seems so odd,
Anything involving satan, can draw me closer to God.
You may yield when tempted, and feel failure brings you shame,
But, when you give into temptation, God loves you
just the same.

The Power of the Tongue

Regardless of how much money you have,
no matter how old or how young,
The struggle is the same for each of us
to control the power of the tongue.
It can really cause you problems
when you don't use it like you should,
Yet it can be your biggest asset
if you use it to only do good.
It's funny how something so small
can play a part so large,
Though the body has many parts
it's the tongue that's still in charge.
It's true the tongue is not the place
where words get their start,
Still, it's the tongue that reveals
what exists inside your heart.
Words can be quite powerful
and the tongue can fan the flame,
You will hurt your fellow man
if your tongue you do not tame.
Be careful before you open your mouth
and let your words freely flow,
You will hurt your family and friends
and even people you don't know.
The tongue reveals both good and bad
regardless of who you're among,

Never underestimate the power you possess
on the tip of your very own tongue.

The Twisted Truth

I'm not sure if there's anything left
that I can one hundred percent believe,
It seems truth no longer matters
and people would rather deceive.
There was a time not long ago
when truth was a valued trait,
Now days when you tell the truth
you subject yourself to hate.
Over time truth's been watered down
and eventually lost its appeal,
I'm not buying into this lie
because that's not the way I feel.
Power, greed, and the love of money
have torn our world apart,
People will do anything to get a share,
and the lies are just a start.
Little by little they twist the truth,
and replace it with a lie,
Eventually lying becomes second nature
and they don't even have to try.
A lie just pops right out of their mouth
its what you expect to hear,
The truth is nowhere to be found
that's one truth that's crystal clear.
A lie cannot tell the truth
and the truth can never lie,
Still, people will try to twist the truth
until the day they die.
Is there a way to get back to truth

and restore integrity in our life,
Can we build trust like we once had
so, we don't cause each other strife.
Well, Jesus is the life, the truth
and friend He's the only way,
We can restore integrity and truth
like we had back in the day.
There's only one thing I can fully believe
and its really quite clear to see,
Trust in God's Word and not in the world
because God has never lied to me.

Trust

Relationships have important needs,
but to me nothing exceeds trust.
It tops my list of needed traits,
and quite simply is a must.
Though there are many other qualities,
we will need along life's way,
Trust stands alone atop the list,
at least that's what I say.
You may agree or maybe not,
but stop and think real hard,
Of the many things in life so far,
a lack of trust has scarred.
A lack of trust can splinter life,
into a thousand little parts,
It breaks the bond that let's love flow,
between two people's hearts.
Just the same, if not betrayed,
then trust becomes the glue,
That binds our hearts together,
knowing I can count on you.
We should love and show respect,
and be kind along the way,
But trust should stand atop the list,
or it all will soon decay.
Remember whoever is in your life,
these words will reign as true,
Nothing is more needed than trust
and it all begins with you.

Section Four

A CHANGING WORLD

For Reflection:

The world is a place of never-ending change, but the way the world is changing now must be some kind of bad dream; I think we've completely lost our minds.

These things have I spoken unto you, that in me ye might have peace. In the world ye shall have tribulation: but be of good cheer; I have overcome the world.

—John 16:33

A Changing World

America the Great

Is America really worth saving
this land I call my home,
A place that's rich in choices
a land where I'm free to roam.
A place I proudly wave my flag
and my voice can still be heard,
A place where I can go to church
and open up God's Holy Word.
A place where things I really need
I don't give a second thought,
Anything I could possibly want
there's a place it can be bought.
My friend, this land I speak of
we truly have it all,
But unless we start protecting it
this great nation soon will fall.
Is America really worth saving
I think you know what answer I'll give,
Just look at other countries
and see how other people live.
It don't take long to realize
America is truly blessed,
It's important we pull together
for we face a rugged test.
With all the freedom we possess
in our sacred land,
We truly are in jeopardy, my friend,
and it's time we make a stand.
It's not just freedom's and privileges

it's our health and children, too,
If we're to save this land we love
it'll be up to me and you.
Yes, America really is worth saving;
it's the greatest place on earth,
So, all hands-on deck, let's pull together,
and save where freedom had its birth.

Breaking Chains

What in the world am I looking at
it seems they've stacked the deck,
It's time to break these liberal chains
they've wrapped around our neck.
First, they take kids' rights in school
and tell them they can't pray,
Then the flag and Pledge of Allegiance,
and they cull what they can say.
What about the parents of children
who are told they have no voice,
When it comes to what they teach our kids
its them that makes that choice.
This liberal ideology
is not confined to just our schools,
No everywhere I go these days
I see these crazy fools.
They kill little babies before they're born,
there is no respect for life,
Heck, a man can have a husband
instead of getting married to a wife.
We no longer can identify
is this a woman or a man,
We're told to open up our minds
and forget about God's plan.
Most any opinion I have these days
they label as a "racial slur",
This craziness happened so fast
it seems its one big blur.
It's time to cast liberal chains aside

and choose to do what's right,
We can never claim our God-given rights
by simply being quiet.
The deck is stacked and the chains are tight
and you may not like your odds,
The choice you have is to stand for truth
or bow down and serve false god's.
It feels wrong to fight for rights
where freedom had its birth,
Yet this is the state of our nation, my friend,
It's time to prove what your freedom's worth.

Confusion Overload

Is what I see what I see
or should what I hear reign *true,*
At first that may sound quite absurd
but listen until I'm through.
You see a girl might be a boy
and a boy may be a girl,
As crazy as that sounds, my friend,
we're living in a crazy world.
It's just a female swimmer they say
but wait isn't that really a male,
You can no longer voice your opinion out loud
for you're too dumb to tell.
Just do as you're told, oh yeah,
you're expected to obey,
It no longer matters about your freedom
or what God's Word has to say.
Try to stand up for the Constitution
or even our Bill of Rights,
You will have stepped across their line,
and they'll have you in their sights.
Don't try to give your opinion,
and certainly don't share a belief,
For once again you've crossed their line
and they'll fill your life with grief.
Educate our children -
it don't seem that way to me,
It's gender roll, drag queen stories,
and a theory called CRT.
It seems we don't want children

to make it to this earth,
We're fighting to take away their life
before they even have their birth.
They're not trying to hide their agenda
their job is no longer hard,
When caught in their own web of lies
they just pull out the "ole race card".
Day after day I see these things
My eyes are open and wide,
But they say I didn't see what I saw
and my freedoms get pushed aside.
Land of the free it certainly is that,
but times are sure getting lean,
Our freedoms are being stomped on
in ways we've never seen.
Don't be a little robot, my friend,
and bow down as you are told,
You know what you see is what you see
so stand up, be brave and bold.
You know I'm right, it's really simple;
it's as clear as day
So, remember the truth is in what you see,
and what God's Word has to say.

National Emergency

Just when you think you've seen it all
you see something that blows your mind,
These days you don't really have to look hard
crazy stuff is easy to find.
No doubt we're a bit confused these days
we're living in a crazy world,
We no longer can identify what a woman is,
and a boy thinks he's a girl.
Are we trying to destroy our great nation
it's getting kind of hard to tell,
Instead of holding criminals accountable
we're letting them out of jail.
The political world has always been corrupt
abusing the power they possess,
Where all the money they've printed is going
I'm afraid that is anybody's guess.
Truth is I don't think we've seen it all
there is surely more to come,
I say that because the leaders we're electing
quite honestly are out and out dumb.
Power, greed, and a love for money
has made us corrupt to the core,
Having good character and doing what's right
doesn't seem to matter anymore.
It's not just politicians, we all have a hand
in causing our great nation to fall,
You probably think after seeing so much
that surely we've seen it all.
I hate to present such a negative picture

when looking at the days ahead,
I hope that things slowly improve,
and won't keep getting worse instead.
My friend, that may not be the case
for we've dug a mighty big hole,
Still, all things are possible with God,
and we know He must play a huge role.
So don't give up, and don't give in,
rely on God to carry you through,
It's a crazy world and there's more to come,
And, yes, it still matters what you do.

Save America

I've always been a proud American,
there's no greater place to be,
The unequaled "Home of the Brave",
land of the hard-fought free.
Yet, things have become quite different
and it seems my feelings have changed,
Although America is still a great country
our people have become so deranged.
I've been known to exaggerate at times
trying to get my point across,
Still, there's no good way to explain it,
I truly am at a loss.
My head is spinning in circles
I'm dizzy from what I keep seeing,
People I once thought were normal
no longer seem like real human beings.
I love America and I'd like to believe
the things I'm seeing aren't true,
Is it just me, have I gone crazy
or do you see the same things too.
There's always been good and evil
there's always been a certain amount of odd,
But people these days do whatever they want
while they spit in the face of God.
Things that are good are viewed as evil
and evil is portrayed as good,
We no longer act as salt and light
though, God's Word clearly says we should.
I never want to see America fall

for this country I feel is so great,
If we don't turn back to God soon, my friend,
I'm afraid it may be too late.
We have become such a divided people
there's division throughout our land,
God's Word tells us a house divided
will never be able to stand.
There's people on the left and people on the right
there's even people in between,
American's have always had different views
but we're looking at a much different scene.
This country was founded with God at the helm
it was He who directed our path,
Along the way we've abandoned God's principles
and we're starting to feel His wrath.
You may think I'm exaggerating my point
about all the changes I see,
Still, if we don't stand up and be brave people
we won't stay the land of the free.
I'm actually surprised at God's patience
as He looks at how far we've strayed,
We abandoned our Constitution and the Bible,
our founding fathers and God perfectly laid.
My friend, it's time we got down on our knees
and invite God back through America's door,
If we don't live by the commandments of God
we can't expect His blessings anymore.
I'm not crazy, and I'm not by myself,
you know what I'm saying is true,

We must turn back to God to save America
and it all starts with me and you.

Soul Control

Are our children little robots
No, they are made of flesh and bone.
We can't act as if they're all the same,
and treat them like little clones.
It was not too awfully long ago
a parent was in full control,
But this no longer seems to be the case
for they now want our children's soul.
That may sound a bit absurd at first,
but, my friend, it really is true,
It's not just the children they're after
they want to capture the parents soul, too.
You may be wondering who is this "they,"
that these words are all about,
Let me help open up your eyes
in case you haven't figured it out.
They are the people who desire power,
and don't want God in control,
So they remove God any way they can
then try to take on His role.
They are the people who rewrite the laws
and take our freedoms away,
They are the ones whose voices are heard
and determine what others can say.
They are the very people who seek
to control every area of your life,
They even want to determine what sex you are

or if a husband can now be a wife.
It really is total chaos, my friend,
and it's only going to get worse,
When you try to play the role of God
you must then face the devil's curse.
Right now the devil is laughing out loud
as He watches this story unfold,
It's important God's people stand together
for the end story hasn't yet been told.
Sometimes it's really hard to tell,
things aren't always as they seem,
Still, remember in the end satan loses
and Christ will reign supreme.
For now protect your little ones,
and protect your own self, too.
Trust in God and keep the faith
when it seems there's nothing you can do.
No matter what they decide to do
to attain their own earthly goal,
All God's people know God's in control
and it's He who owns our soul.

To Tell the Truth

To tell the truth, I am amazed when I see how people act,
Information offered these days contains more fiction than fact.
When I was a young boy, living in my father's house,
I learned to tell the truth to my dad and to his spouse.
Your word's important, it'll get you far, I remember he
said to me,
To tell the truth, now that years have passed, I'll admit I
must agree.
I kept my word at times, with important things at stake,
I got by on just my word, along with a firm handshake.
People should understand the importance of integrity today,
To tell the truth, I look around, and it hasn't worked
out that way.
As time goes on, I can clearly see, the truth gets watered down,
To tell the truth, when I offer my word, people look at me
and frown.
No need for that, they lend a pen and a contract I can sign,
My firm handshake does no good, unless I sign on the
dotted line.
I better be careful what I sign, really shows my true intent,
My word no longer matters, it's the nature of the small
fine print.
People want money and power, and that leads to selfish greed,
To tell the truth, I am mighty thankful, I don't feel that's
what I need.
The lesson I learned from days gone by, to how things are
these days,
Is not to allow what others do, to influence me, to
change my ways.

It's still a firm handshake, and my word still reigns supreme,
To tell the truth, I can keep my integrity, and still live the
"American Dream."

What's Wrong with America

It's become a touchy subject I'll admit
you must be careful what words you say,
Don't use a word that's not approved
or they might take your job away.
That sentence is a perfect example
it's sad, but yet it's true,
I broke the code by saying "they"
in the words I just spoke to you.
It has become quite obvious
things aren't like they once were,
Now-a-days everything is a gender breech
or is deemed a racial slur.
People are no doubt disrespectful
and some people have bad intent,
If we allow these things to happen
the wrong message is being sent.
Still, it's going a bit overboard
when it takes others freedoms away,
It seems to me that's where we are
In the good ole USA.
I want to respect your rights, my friend,
I want mine respected, too.
When you infringe upon my rights
it's hard to have respect for you.
There's two sides to every story,
each side thinks theirs makes sense,
Then there's those that are afraid to offend
who are always riding the fence.
We have some things available

to help these problems go away,
Stop stepping on the Constitution,
then open up your Bible and pray.
When you take God out of the equation
it just goes downhill from there,
It's happening all around us
and not enough people seem to care.
I don't want to minimize our past
and the hardships people had to face,
Still, as a whole we've come together
and our problem is not about race.
It's not about gender identity
or what sex you claim to be,
Those are distractions from our so called leaders,
they are pushing on you and me.
It's about turning our back on God
and trying to take on His role,
Little by little we've abandoned God
and we're spiraling out of control.
You see without God at the helm
evil takes our God given rights away,
It's not a sustainable course
and there's a high price America will pay.
I know it's a touchy subject
that's what I said right from the start,
But it's time to push back against evil
and instill God's principles back in our heart.
Freedom is never freedom, my friend,
when you take others freedoms away,

That's exactly the problem we're facing
in the world we live in today.
There will always be people with bad intent
who disrespect others with what they say,
But we can't let that change our great country
and allow our freedoms to be taken away.

You Are What You Are

Thank you, ma'am or sir, I'm not quite sure
which one I'm talking to,
This used to be a simple task,
but these days I have no clue.
You may think that sounds crazy,
and I'm overstating my case,
But it's the truth, because you can't tell
by just looking at someone's face.
Both men and women seem confused
about which sex they really are,
I don't know about you, my friend,
but to me that's just bizarre.
How can a man become a woman,
or a woman become a man,
You simply are what you are,
created by God's own hand.
It's true you can be anything you want,
that's part of the American dream,
Yet you've lost your way if you believe
you can become whatever sex you deem.
I'm not trying to judge the people
who want to live life that way,
I'm just here to inform those folks
about what God's Word has to say.
The Bible says God made man and woman,
and God never makes mistakes,
When you try to change how God made you,
You're living your life as fakes.
I know this kind of straight-talk

makes the "woke mob" mighty mad,
Still, a man simply can't be a mom,
and a woman can't be a dad.
Enjoy your freedom and enjoy your life,
and be all that you can be
I'll do the same the way God designed it,
just don't push your nonsense on me.

Section Five

STORY TIME

For Reflection:

Combine the reality of God's love and a creative mind, and you get stories that move your heart as you laugh, cry, and think about the goodness of God.

For thou, Lord, art good, and ready to forgive; and plenteous in mercy unto all them that call upon thee.

—Psalm 86:5

Story Time

A Soul Revived

A helpless soul lies waiting
in a hospital bed,
The body is still living,
it's the soul that is dead.
Not an unusual scene,
it's much like any other,
Except for I know the family
and the patient's younger brother.
They watch as Wade's life
slowly starts slipping away,
They all pray for a miracle
for they know there's no other way.
The younger brother is restless
as he sits by Wade's bed,
Still, he knows it's his brother's soul
he should be concerned for, instead.
As the situation grows darker,
a decision must be made,
Should the tube be removed
from the dying body of Wade.
The vital signs weakened,
the time now had drawn nigh,
When they remove the tubes,
would his brother just die?
So, the younger brother Shannon
knelt down by his side,
And ask his brother Wade
if he knew why Jesus had died.
He asked if he wanted Jesus

to come live in his heart,
Then he shared the sinner's prayer
and Wade managed to do his part.
The moment the prayer ended
a miracle seemed to take place,
The monitor suddenly stopped beeping
and Wade's heartbeat changed its pace.
I guess it goes without saying
this left Shannon floored,
Although he knew miracles happen
when you truly trust in the Lord.
Now Shannon and all his family
are glad Wade's still alive,
It's clear the hand of God
is what made his heart revive.
But that's not the story's end
no, my friend, it's only the start,
For now Wade has Jesus Christ
alive inside his heart.
All because his brother Shannon
chose to extend his hand,
he shared the love of Jesus
and God's salvation plan.
Now the two brothers can rejoice
as they share the love of the Lord,
With a miracle story to tell
I'm sure they'll never be bored.
Wade's vital signs are better
his soul's been saved from hell,

he's been baptized and redeemed
and he's doing pretty well.
As for Shannon, he's by his brother's side,
he helps when there's a need,
And he's reaping what he boldly planted
because God has watered his seed.

A Sweet Dream

Tired from the night shift, my eyes were heavy, I desperately
needed some sleep,
I unlocked my front door and stumbled thru the darkness, then
fell on my bed in a heap.
The sun made its entrance, across the morning sky, a scene I
never would see,
I love a good sunrise, but for the moment, my sleep was
important to me.
My head on the pillow, it didn't take long, before I was out
like a light,
But 'lo and behold, while deep in my sleep, I saw a
magnificent sight.
There was Jesus, knocking on my front door, and for a moment
I was outside my dream,
I awoke in a sweat, delirious and confused, but I was sure it was
Jesus I'd seen.
Now wide awake, I scanned my brain, as I sat at the foot
of my bed,
If I could only remember, when I opened the door, what it was
that Jesus had said.
I was really tired, my mind grew weary, and I soon fell asleep
once more,
'Lo and behold, it didn't take long before Jesus was back
at my door.
Expecting Him, I didn't wake up, instead I invited Him in,
But I wasn't prepared to meet Him in person, and I didn't know
where to begin.
The silence was deafening, but after some time, Jesus looked
and said with a smile,

Don't worry my son, there's no need to talk, I just came to sit
for a while.
I sat in awe and wondered why, it was for me that Jesus cares,
Suddenly, I realized Jesus had come, because of what I had said
in my prayers.
Just as quickly as I'd gone to sleep, I awoke and sat up
in my bed,
Though Jesus spoke only one sentence, I knew He had meant
what He said.
I struggled with my dream, but I couldn't understand, no matter
how hard I tried,
So, still half asleep, I went to my front door, and took a quick
look outside.
There stood Jesus watering my flowers, it was Him, I
couldn't be wrong,
In a moment of clarity, it suddenly hit me that Jesus was there
all along.
Whether I am sleeping, or I'm wide awake, no matter
where I may go,
There beside me is my Jesus, though His face He may choose
not to show.
Wow, what a morning, I felt truly blessed, for Jesus had
revealed His face,
He knocked on my front door, sat for a while, and
first-hand delivered His grace.
I watched as Jesus watered my flowers, then He said with that
same glorious smile,
I guess I should go, I have others to see, and you'll be good
for a while.

Then I lost sight of His glorious face, but even though it was not there to see,
Jesus had shown me through a sweet dream, that He would always be there for me.

Bible All-Stars

I had a really grand idea,
it came to me in a dream,
I was coaching a group of all-stars
with only Bible characters on the team.
Jesus was my general manager
He was in charge of playing time,
He always made out the lineup
and decided who "rode the pine".
Maybe you think it's not a problem
and the chemistry will be all good,
The fact they're all Bible characters
kind of suggest to me it should.
But, my friend, this is a co-ed team
there are men and women too,
There's bound to be some arguing
because that's what men and women do.
Don't act surprised, you know it's true,
that's the way it is today,
Especially when it comes to an all-star team
where everybody believes they should play.
That's why Jesus is my general manager,
and I just coach during the game,
If the line-up is not productive
I let Jesus take the blame.
Don't get upset with me, my friend,
thinking I give Jesus guilt,
Jesus is used to taking the blame

and that's how His team is built.
You may think this team's dysfunctional
but that's really not the case,
If the players get too out of hand
Jesus will put them in their place.
When it comes down to game day
the arguing goes out the door,
Both the men and women pull together,
and they don't bicker anymore.
All the players on my team
know Jesus from long ago,
They know from past experiences
they should let Jesus run the show.
As for me, I'm having fun coaching
this Bible All-Star team,
As long as Jesus is my general manager
it should work out just like my dream.

Cowboy Jesus

If Jesus was really a cowboy
I'd have to get another horse,
I'm not sure my cowboy habits
have me riding a Jesus course.
I'd put on my best belt buckle
and buy a ten gallon hat,
Then I'd gather around the campfire
so I could sit where Jesus sat.
I'd put on my best pair of boots
with the cowboy spurs intact,
Then I'd take off all my gun belts
and I'd polish up my act.
I'd build a new corral for him
to keep his horse at night,
I'd give him his own bunk house
where He'd have nothing there but quiet.
I'd tell all my old ranch hands
to check their ego at the door,
Getting liquored up and fighting
won't be allowed here anymore.
No more dance hall girls on weekends
like you've grown accustomed to,
No more stayin out till sunrise
your hell raisin days are through.
As for me, I've taken off my gun belts
and I've shined up all my boots,
I've dedicated my whole ranch to Jesus,
it's time for him to see my fruits.
No more roamin on the open range

and trying to run my ranch alone,
I've already created enough problems
from the bad seeds I have sown.
It's time to ride and rope for Jesus
and live the way He'd want me to,
For Jesus if you were really a cowboy
I'd want to look more like you do.
Now I'll always be a cowboy
but my ranch won't ever be the same,
I'm no longer rustling cattle
or playing the bar room game.
I'm branding all my cattle for Jesus,
I'm even using His watering hole,
No more playing crooked poker
I'm giving back all the money I stole.
I'm mending all my fences
and wearing my Jesus brand real proud,
I'm posting signs all around my ranch
saying, "only clean cowboys allowed."
It's a new saddle I'll be riding
and it will take some breakin in,
I'm sure that won't be a problem
if I trust Jesus, my cowboy friend.
If Jesus was really a cowboy
He'd be the sheriff of my heart,
As long as He's in my bunkhouse
I'm gonna do my cowboy part.
What's my part, well, it's your part, too;
stop doing the things that please us.

Clean up your ranch and clean up your act
and try to look more like cowboy Jesus.
I know Jesus isn't really a cowboy
I'm simply trying to make a point,
You can't rope and ride for Jesus
if you're stinkin up the joint.
So whatever walk of life you're from
remember, it's just a fact,
Jesus can never use you, my friend,
unless you're willing to clean up your act.

Dream Journey through the Bible

I've always been a dreamer,
I dream almost every night,
I dream from the time I close my eyes
until I see the morning light.
I don't always remember what I dream
though they often seem quite real,
Sometimes they are so true to life,
dreams change the way I feel.
I remember last night's dream so well
I'd like to share what I dreamed,
I met the Bible's greatest men,
at least that's the way it seemed.
It began with God's greatest servant
who stood above them all,
I took a stroll through the Bible
walking beside the Apostle Paul.
He made it clear he wasn't around
when some of these stories took place.
Yet, he wanted to share them all with me
to fully explain God's grace.
First, Paul took me to the Garden of Eden
to show where we fall prey to sin,
he told me to enjoy the beautiful sight
for we'd never be here again.
Then we started on our journey,
he showed me Bible heroes and kings,
There's no way I can share them all
I saw far too many things.
However, I do remember Moses and Noah

Abraham and Isaac his son,
I met so many descendants of these great men
I can't remember everyone.
I met many kings some good, some bad,
still a couple stood out to me,
King Solomon and King David were Godly men
I'm sure glad I got to see.
All the prophets gathered around
and Paul led us in a prayer,
They knew Paul was from the New Testament
yet they didn't seem to care.
I asked the prophets all about God
and honestly I wanted to stay,
But Paul motioned me to follow him
and once again we were on our way.
We walked a while until we came to a chasm
one I'd often heard about,
Paul said this was the most likely place
where people started having doubt.
We were crossing from the old to the new
we'd be in a completely different place,
he said I'd probably better understand
once I saw Jesus face-to-face.
I guess since Paul knew God so well
one request was all it took.
Before I knew it, we were across the chasm
walking in the New Testament book.
First, Paul introduced me to the four gospels
Matthew, Mark, Luke, and John,

he said to trust God's reliable word
not the Watchtower or the Quran.
Then Paul took me to meet the disciples.
Jesus chose to fish for men,
I listened to them and I listened to Jesus
tell how the world was broken by sin.
I listened intently as Jesus told the disciples
how their goal was to bring God glory,
I understood that was God's plan
and Jesus's death was part of the story.
I met lots of people and some of Paul's friends
some good, some bad, and some odd,
Most importantly I learned all about Jesus
and how He was one with my God.
I learned of His love, mercy, and grace
I learned how He died for me,
Not only that, but I learned that salvation
is a gift from God that is free.
I learned Jesus's blood spanned the chasm
and provided forgiveness for sin,
God left behind His story through the prophets
how one day He would come back again.
I'm not sure why God gave me this dream
and you may think this all sounds absurd,
But I saw it in a dream, I see it in the Bible
and I'm making sure God's story gets heard.

Eye in the Sky

I stumbled into a surveillance room
one that's never been seen,
There were huge screens and little ones to
and every size in between.
These screens were literally everywhere
a million or maybe more,
In hopes I hadn't alarmed anyone
I quietly closed the door.
As I began to walk around the room
I felt this aura in the air,
Up in the distance among the screens
set this unbelievably humongous chair.
I must admit my curiosity had peaked
for the room was a magnificent sight,
This chair was smack dab in the middle
giving off an incredible light.
The light grew dim and the chair spun around,
and much to my surprise,
There was Jesus smiling at me
He was looking dead into my eyes.
I could feel Jesus looking into my soul
I was shaking from head to toe,
I was so overwhelmed I wanted to run,
but there was nowhere for me to go.
It took a minute, but I gathered myself
I remembered Jesus was my friend,
Though it wasn't clear why I was here
I knew this wasn't my end.
Jesus reached over and flicked a switch

and the screens suddenly had sound,
He took my hand gently in His
and started to lead me around.
With only the love Jesus could show
He took me through all of the screens,
I was made aware of the good and bad
He saw in each of the scenes.
It seemed as though I stumbled into this room
but Jesus was making it clear,
His purpose was to give me a glimpse of my life
and that's why He had brought me here.
Now it all made sense to me
I knew Jesus truly did care,
He led me back to the center of the room
and He sat back down in His chair.
Then Jesus smiled at me again
and His chair spun around once more,
His incredible light filled up the room
as I made my way back to the door.
I opened the door and took one last glance
and for a moment I stood there and cried,
Then once again I gathered myself
and walked through to the other side.
Somehow, I knew Jesus had opened that door
to instill down deep in my heart,
That He had things to accomplish through me
and it was important that I do my part.
There's a million screens or maybe more
that Jesus is watching of you,

He sees the good things you have done
and He sees the bad things too.
Take it from someone who's been thru the door
and taken the whole grand tour,
Jesus revealed a message to me
it's the same for you, I'm sure.
He has a purpose for each of our lives
and He's watching our every step,
He's always at the center of our room
if we should ever need any help.
You may never stumble in a room full of screens
and see Jesus lit up in a chair,
But rest assured He has a purpose for your life
and know that He truly does care.

Far Away Land

Once upon a time, my friend,
in a land far, far away,
The doors were left unlocked at night
and the children went outside to play.
Doing good to others was valued
and polished like it was gold,
Respect was just a common trait
from young folk toward the old.
Sunday morning church was something
almost every family did,
For parents in this far away land
really cared about their kid.
You may think this land I speak of
is miles away in outer space,
Yet sadly enough, it's right beside you,
right here is that faraway place.
We're far away from values we treasured
we've completely gotten out of touch,
We're far away from respecting others
in this land we love so much.
We're far away from truth and reality
things are perverted and down-right odd,
The reason we've gotten to a land far away
is we've gotten far away from God.
Is it possible for us to ever return
to this land far, far away,
You know the land of milk and honey
we proudly call the USA.
Unless we truly humble ourselves

and admit God is what we need,
We'll continue to live in this wretched place
filled with sinful lust and greed.
How about you, my friend, do you long
for that land far away,
Where the doors are left unlocked at night
and the children go outside to play.
Or are you happy in this current place
seeking out your sinful lusts,
I guess the question you must answer
is where will you put your trust.
Now I understand the land far away
has many problems of its own,
Still, the farther we've strayed away from God
the fewer good seeds we have sown.
So I'm on my knees and praying to God
that He'll restore our far away land,
With just our human powers we're doomed
but with the help of God we can.
If you've decided worldly lusts
are not whats most important to you today,
You believe God can restore the far away land
where the children go outside to play.
Then stop for a moment and bow your head
and let's all join hand in hand,
Let's pray together for God to restore us
to our far, far away land

God's Little Helper

I saw this little old lady struggling
to hold open the hospital door,
To manage the door and her wheelchair
seemed for her too big of a chore.
I rushed over to give her a hand
and flashed a big smile on my face,
Somehow I pushed the wrong button
and she quickly put me in my place.
She yelled she didn't need any help
and for me to get out of her way,
I was taken aback, in shock I guess,
and I didn't know what to say.
Maybe she needed to prove to herself,
and perhaps to everybody else too,
Just because she was in a wheelchair
she could still do what she needed to do.
She seemed angry, though I wasn't sure why,
for I'd never seen her before,
Still, somehow she managed the task,
and she wheeled herself through the door.
Several times she glanced over at me,
and for the moment I returned to my seat,
I was truly amazed this little old lady
had pulled off such an amazing feat.
She still seemed very agitated,
as she checked herself in with the nurse,
Then it looked like she needed help again,
when she clumsily dropped her purse.
For whatever reason she didn't get mad,

and she gladly allowed me to assist,
After what had happened a moment ago,
I clearly expected her to resist.
But she didn't, so I handed her the purse,
I handed her a little Bible too,
I told her it was to brighten her day,
and a reminder that Jesus loves you.
She looked up with tears in her eyes,
as she managed her best little smile,
She said I know Jesus and I used to go to church,
but I haven't been in a while.
Years ago when I went to church
I felt so all alone,
I felt I was closer to Jesus
whenever I just stayed at home.
So, I decided to stay at home,
and have church all by myself,
But now my Bible is collecting dust
sitting on my bedroom shelf.
Eventually I forgot about Jesus,
and decided God wasn't even there,
It saddened me because I used to feel
like I wasn't alone in this chair.
I really miss Jesus beside me,
and I'd like to fill that reed,
I'm glad God put you in my path today,
and you have replanted that seed.
Young man you have shown me compassion,
and this Bible just may be the start,

Of me going to church again,
and letting Jesus back into my heart.
As you can imagine, I was quite moved,
by what the old lady had said,
Though they called my name for the doctor,
I stayed with the old lady instead.
We talked and laughed waiting for her appointment,
but that is not where this story ends,
I invited her to go to my church
and we soon became very close friends.
We dusted off that Bible on her shelf
she'd put there many years before,
She now reads it daily and there's no time
for it to collect dust anymore.
She says she's the happiest she's ever been,
and finding Jesus again was the key,
Now she never misses going to church
it's her most favorite place to be.
And me, well, I just keep going to visit,
and helping whenever she needs,
It's a reminder to me every time I visit
that God always waters His seeds.

God's Little Miracle

I'll never forget that fateful day
walking in that hospital room,
Friends and family were gathered around
and you could sense the certain doom.
A young boy, just ten-years-old,
lay in that hospital bed,
he had tubes attached everywhere
and a bandage wrapped around his head.
From the look on all the faces
I knew there was nothing I could say,
So I ask the mother and father
if they'd like for me to pray.
They both nodded their approval
and everyone lowered their head,
I realized these people felt helpless
no matter what words I said.
I lay my hands on the little boy's body
as he lay there helpless and still,
Then I prayed for a miracle from heaven
according to the Heavenly Fathers will.
Somehow God gave me the perfect words
for the family to hear that day,
They dried their tears and hugged my neck
and I soon was on my way.
For I was just a simple Chaplain
who was there to do my part,
Still, somehow I felt the boy would live
I had this feeling deep in my heart.
Days later while headed to another room

I passed by the young boys door,
There was an undeniable feeling in my heart
there was no doom in the room anymore.
I tried to get a grip on myself
as I hurried on down the hall,
For another family was counting on me
and I had to make this call.
I consoled the family and said a prayer
like I'd done many times before,
Then I ran back down the hall
and knocked on the young boys door.
The door opened and there stood the father
he had a twinkle in his eyes,
Across the room I saw the little boy
he was smiling and seemed surprised.
I never thought I'd see you again
the little boy happily said,
A couple of days ago when you prayed for me
mister I was almost dead.
I felt you put your hand on me
then God put His hand on top,
Right before you said that prayer for me
my little heartbeat tried to stop.
Then you spoke those words and God proclaimed
my son, your life is not yet through,
I'm going to keep your little heart beating
I have a special task for you.
I was overjoyed with what I saw
but I couldn't get out a word,

I knew the family's prayers were answered
and a miracle had surely occurred.
It's been twenty years or more now
since God healed that little boy,
I know his mother and father well
and he's still their pride and joy.
That little boy is now a man
and I've grown old and gray,
Still, I will never forget the miracle
God performed on him that day.
And remember the special task God said
He saved the little boy to do,
Well, he works in that same hospital
and he's now a Chaplain, too.

Left Behind

Wow! The sun is already a factor
on this Independence day,
People arrive from everywhere
and boats fill up the bay.
The local pub is jumping
with live music from the band,
I soak it in as I lie back
and dig my toes into the sand.
Children are running and playing
and the beach is getting full,
My comfort zone is off the chart
still I feel the oceans pull.
I know I can't resist the call
I was never one to behave
I grab my favorite surf board
hit the water and pick a wave.
The surf was up so I had some fun
then I headed back to shore,
I couldn't help but notice
there weren't as many people as before.
I'd been gone less than an hour
so the scene seemed really odd,
Then I heard some lady screaming
how she wish that she knew God.
It suddenly hit me all at once
that this scene I had captured,
Was because the Lord had returned
and some people had been raptured.
As the truth set in, people panicked,

and some started losing their mind.
Again it hit me all at once
that I'd been left behind.
If only I had listened that day
when the preacher came by our house,
he shared the story of Jesus
with both me and my spouse.
My wife decided to listen,
she thought this Jesus thing was real,
She got saved and went to church
and tried to live within God's will.
I took a different route than her
I didn't want Jesus in my life,
So, I filed for a divorce
and I found another wife.
Don't get me wrong, I had some problems
but I thought life was pretty grand,
Right up to today on the beach
when I dug my toes into the sand.
A sinking feeling settled in
I had failed to do my part,
I had sold out to the devil,
and shut Jesus out of my heart.
The preacher said this day would come,
but I mocked and made up jokes,
I was busy going to the pub
drinking beer and taking tokes.
A little fun never hurt no one
that's what I'd always say,

The road to hell's mighty wide
and now it seems, I'm on my way.
That's just how fast it will happen
when Jesus makes His return,
So, give your heart to Him today,
otherwise your soul will burn.
No matter how many good deeds you do
how often your helpful and kind,
Unless you give your heart to Jesus
it is you who'll be left behind.

Making Memories

A young boy bound out of bed
with a joy money just can't buy,
he raced outside to embrace the day
as the sun rose across the sky.
It was a day he'd long awaited
to celebrate his new age,
he was now an official teenager
and he was ready to turn a new page.
It was the most beautiful day he'd ever seen
as he looked out across the bay,
For twelve long years, he'd rolled out of bed
looking forward to this very day.
His dad had always promised him
this special day would soon arrive,
When they hit the open waves that day
the family boat would be his to drive.
To some it may not seem a big deal
still the boys heart swelled with pride,
For today he was the official captain
and this was no ordinary ride.
It was a special bond created by dad
placing the key in his son's hand,
As he cranked the boat he briefly felt
like he had just become a real man.
Was just one of many special memories
this boy had with dad out at sea,
I know how special those memories are
because that little boy was me.
Though I am no longer a teenage boy

I still keep in touch with my dad,
We reminisce of my first captain's ride
and other great memories we've had.
The lesson I learned from my dad
I'd like to pass along to you,
Is your creating memories for a lifetime
in everything you choose to do.
So, choose wisely the things you share,
and be proud of the seeds you've sown,
Then you'll have a lifetime of memories to share
once your children are out on their own.

Miraculous Day

I was looking for a miracle today
as I opened up my eyes,
I reeled back my window shades
and looked into God's beautiful skies.
Just across the far horizon
the sun peered back at me,
There was nothing but perfect blue skies
as far as I could see.
The water was as smooth as glass
out across the bay,
God was showing me His wonders
with this magnificent display.
I rubbed the sleep from my eyes,
and took a walk outside,
Then I stopped and said a prayer,
and ask God to be my guide.
I didn't know where He'd lead me,
but I knew He had a plan,
I felt a peace inside my heart
knowing I was in God's hand.
I soaked up all the sunshine
then I heard a small still voice,
God was guiding me as I had asked
He was even giving me a choice.
A bit unusual I will admit
That's not usually what I hear,
God was giving a choice to me
He made that very clear.
I went inside and dressed myself,

and off to church I went,
I was going to attend a different church
for that's what God had clearly meant.
My choice was to attend my old church
or go and find a new church door,
I decided to find a new church,
and see what God might have in store.
Which new church I should attend
I really did not know,
So I let the Holy Spirit guide me,
and show me where my car should go.
I wound up at this little country church,
one I've never seen before.
I parked my car, and grabbed my Bible,
and walked inside the door.
If I told you everything I saw
you probably would not believe,
For the presence of God was everywhere,
and I was happy to receive
Just good ole folks and lots of children
singing and praising God's name,
By the time I left the church that day
I knew I'd never be the same.
My heart kept getting blessed over and over
by the music and sermon as well,
But, there's one particular thing that occurred,
that I'd really like to tell.
After a dozen songs were sung,
I'm not kidding, maybe more,

The pastor, an eighty-year-old man,
got up and paced across the floor.
He wasn't preaching, he was just thanking,
people in the church as a whole,
he called out people one by one
professing how they had blessed his soul.
Then he pointed to this little old lady
who was sitting right across the aisle,
With tears in his eyes he thanked her
at the same time flashing a smile.
He asked her to come to the front,
and bless the church with her voice,
She slowly stepped away from her seat
it didn't seem she had much of a choice.
She was a colored lady, all bent over,
she could barely walk down the aisle,
Still, she made her way to the altar
although it certainly took her a while.
Remember that miracle I spoke of
back at the start of my day,
How I had asked God to guide me
when I bowed my head to pray.
Well here was my miracle, a little old lady,
who could barely make it around,
Yet, when she opened her mouth to sing,
she let out the most angelic sound.
She sang "His Name is Wonderful,' a popular song,
one I've heard many times before,
It was as if the heavens had opened

I couldn't hold back my tears anymore.
I've seen mega churches with huge choirs,
and heard solos sung by the best,
Yet, the angelic sound from this old lady
put my soul at perfect rest.
Maybe for you it doesn't seem special,
for you didn't hear her voice,
But that's not the point of the story,
it's about trying to make the right choice.
See, if we ask God to guide our steps,
and we always follow His lead,
He will bless us in the most beautiful way,
and give us exactly the miracle we need.

Misguided Religion

What I was doing seemed so significant
yet no one really appeared to care,
So, I slipped in and found a seat
and sat down to say a prayer.
It was almost like being in a bubble
for I could hardly hear a sound,
I felt like I was all alone
even though people were all around.
I sat quietly on that cold church pew
wondering why I'd ever been born,
For I noticed people staring at me
with my clothes all dirty and torn.
I felt ashamed and wanted to leave
but, I seemed frozen to my seat,
I knew I'd come for just one reason,
it was Jesus I had to meet.
It was getting harder not to notice
as more people began to stare,
There was no doubt I wasn't welcome
and I forgot about my prayer.
Then it happened as I had feared,
I heard a voice boldly say,
Hey son, you're in God's house now,
you can't come here dressed that way.
I was no longer in a bubble
I was crushed by what I heard,
I got up no longer frozen to my pew
and fled the church without a word.
As I ran across the parking lot

my eyes were filled with tears,
It was the farthest I'd ever felt from God
in all my many years.
I had no shoes upon my feet
still I ran with all my might,
Determined not to turn around
until the church was no longer
in sight.
Now miles away I finally stopped
and dried the tears from my eyes,
Then I looked up towards the heavens
and I suddenly felt my spirits rise.
For there with no one else around
with the church nowhere in sight,
I felt the loving arms of Jesus
reach from heaven and hold me tight.
With no one to tell me how to dress
and no people to stop and stare,
I rested in the arms of my Jesus
and I offered up my prayer.
I knew Jesus had heard my prayer
and then I heard Jesus say,
My son, it's sinful that people in church
so often treat my children this way.
It matters not if you have shoes
or if you have nice clothes to wear,
You are always welcome in the house of God
to offer me up your prayer.
From this day forward if you enter a church

and you don't feel a warm embrace,
Don't feel ashamed just quietly leave
and go find another place.
You'll know you've found the right church
when the people's number one goal,
It's not the clothes you are wearing my child
but it's the status of your soul.

Real Life Movie

God's the screenwriter of my life,
Jesus is the star of the show,
The Holy Spirit is my director,
He tells me where I should go.
This is not some Hollywood show,
it's a real life movie, my friend.
I'll tell you about this amazing plot,
so listen up till the very end.
In the beginning long ago
God created both heaven and earth,
As time went on He sent His Son
through an amazing virgin birth.
Jesus was His appointed name
He was a man yet He was God,
The sins of the world were put on Him,
it was a painful path He trod.
Still, He lived a perfect sinless life
then He died for you and I,
He arose again and ascended to heaven
to reign with His Father in the sky.
There were many stories too many to tell
that led up to this crucifixion story,
But Jesus was the star of the show
and we want Him to get all the glory.
Now fast forward several thousand years
God's masterful plot is still in place,
Only now it's you and I, my friend,
who are experiencing God's amazing grace.
Through Bible times and all those years

God has written this masterful plot,
I'm a part of God's perfect story
He's put me in this specific spot.
I'm no Noah, Moses, or Abraham
I'm not a prophet or a king,
Still, God made a special role for me
to do a very important thing.
I'm not exactly sure where I should go
but the Holy Spirit will be my guide,
I know Jesus is the star of the show
and He is always by my side.
I'm here to remind people about Jesus
and His story from long ago,
I'm here to share the gift of salvation
it's a story everyone needs to know.
My friend, it's an incredible story
that started now centuries ago,
God's the screenwriter and Jesus is the star
but we all have a part in this show.
Maybe you don't know your exact role
and you're not sure what lines you should say,
Keep listening to the director, my friend,
and the Holy Spirit will show you the way.

Sharing Jesus

I stopped and talked to a man today
who was sitting on the side of the road,
It only took one look into his eyes
to see he carried a heavy load.
I ask him if he knew Jesus
and he said he knew Him well,
But the spirit told me something was wrong
and I should sit and stay a spell.
It didn't take me very long
before I could clearly see,
The chains that had him shackled
and what he needed to be free.
He was buried beneath guilt and shame
from a long, long time ago,
The devil was holding him captive
so his faith could never grow.
He really shared his heart with me
and we talked for quite a while,
Yet, I wondered if he really knew Jesus
for he never even cracked a smile.
So, I dug a little deeper
to see if I could find his joy,
For he said that he had known Jesus
since he was a very young boy,
I wasn't trying to judge the man
my motive was clean and pure,
I wanted to know Jesus was in his heart
and it was clear that he wasn't sure.
It was obvious he knew who Jesus was

and he had for many years,
Yet when I asked, if Jesus lived in his heart,
he could no longer hold back his tears.
It seemed my new friend knew Jesus
and he believed that God was real,
But, he'd never ask Jesus into his heart,
to solidify the deal.
I explained how eternal life could be his
and it was Christ who suffered the loss,
I told him salvation was his free gift
because Jesus died for him on the cross.
He understood and said he really got it
as he smiled and wiped away his tears,
Then he said a prayer and accepted Jesus
and gave him all his guilt and fears.
Something important I've learned over time
it matters what questions you ask,
I want to be sure people follow Jesus
and here's how I accomplish that task.
I follow up and always make sure
when I ask if people know Jesus,
Because many people really believe they do
and others just pretend trying to please us.
You see, my friend, you never know for sure
if it's that person's last day on earth,
You want them to know they really know Jesus
and understand what their soul's really worth.
It may not be a man you talk to
and it may not be on the side of the road,

Still, know wherever you are when you share Jesus
you're helping someone to lighten their load.

Smash Up Derby

I always wanted my own car
so, I worked and saved up some cash,
I was finally able to get what I wanted
but it didn't take me long to crash.
I scrimped and saved every penny I earned
and I vowed to change my luck,
This time instead of buying a car
I thought I'd just buy me a truck.
I finally found one that met my eye
and I laid down my hard earned cash,
The same thing happened, it didn't take long
before I had another crash.
I was crushed and so was my truck
it was upside down in a ditch,
This was posing a pretty big problem
because brother, I'm just not that rich.
So, I went to the bank and took out a loan
I promised I would pay it back,
But, I was so busy earning money
somehow I must have lost track.
I bought a car with the money
and I bought a motorcycle too,
Now the bank was taking them back
and I wasn't sure what to do.
I needed a ride to get to work
yet the job wasn't paying the bills,
Anyone who's been in this predicament,
you know exactly how this feels.
I kept scratching, scrapping, and saving

I even rode a bicycle to work,
It didn't cost much and I got in shape
and that was a nice little perk.
Time drug on for a couple of years
I kept putting money away,
I desperately wanted another ride
I could hardly wait for the day.
It seemed like forever but it finally came
I'd saved enough money once again,
I went to the dealer and picked out a ride
and took it out for a spin.
Next thing I knew, I woke up in the hospital.
I was wearing a full body cast,
I wasn't sure exactly how it happened
but I knew once again I had crashed.
For several months I lay in bed
wondering why this kept happening to me,
The longer I thought the clearer it got
in fact it became easy to see.
It didn't matter what I was driving
I was driving it way too fast,
I never had time to avoid disaster
that's why I'd always crashed.
Good thing I discovered the problem
because it was costing me an arm and a leg,
I've never like borrowing from the bank
and I sure don't want to have to beg.
So, these days I just putt along
I don't worry because I'm getting passed,

I just smile and wave as people fly by
knowing I won't be the one who crashed.

The Cliché Parade

Here's a little poem with some old clichés
kind of like a blast from the past,
This is your chance to be a back seat driver
buckle up 'cause it's gonna go fast.
Hope I didn't bite off more than I can chew
I've got a way with words every now and again,
So without further ado let's break a leg
and let the cliché parade begin.
There is no rainbow without a cloud and a storm
at least that's how the old saying goes,
You must faithfully water a seed, my friend,
to enjoy watching how much it grows.
You can't have your cake and eat it too
yet we all seem to give it a try,
People never know how much they are loved
if you don't tell them before they die.
What don't kill you only makes you stronger
I suppose that saying is true,
So is two wrongs don't make a right
no matter what two wrongs you may do.
Actions speak louder than words for sure
although words seem to hold their own,
Any job worth doing is worth doing well
is usually not learned till we're grown.
God helps those who help themselves
that's not exactly the words God spoke,
The early bird always gets the worm
and he's the one the worm just might choke.
There's no such thing as a free lunch

that saying is a bit out of date,
What's done is done while certainly true
doesn't mean it has sealed your fate.
Don't put all your eggs in one basket
we all know what that saying means,
Everything in life happens for a reason
at least that's the way it seems.
Put your money where your mouth is
we all know talk is cheap,
We certainly know God was right when He said
what you sow is what you ll reap.
If you snooze you lose, no pain no gain
both are great motivational tools,
Don't try to judge a book by its cover
for this is the practice of fools.
If it ain't broke then don t fix it
what a novel little thought,
Patience is a virtue in life
one that is very highly sought.
Laughter is the best medicine
I've found this usually is the case,
You can bet that misery loves company
and boy what a toxic place.
People in glass houses shouldn't throw stones
or else they'll break their own glass,
Where there's a will there is a way
and only losers look for a free pass.
Everyone knows knowledge is power
it's the beginning of wisdom as well,

Necessity is the mother of invention
those who've been there have a story to tell.
It's true all that glitters isn't gold
we've all learned this lesson before,
Business before pleasure is a good practice
though for most it seems quite a chore.
You can fly off the handle if you'd like
or better yet fly by the seat of your pants,
But don't jump from the frying pan into the fire
for I'm sure you won't enjoy that dance.
It's long been understood a man's home is his castle
and a penny saved is a penny earned,
You can save a big nest egg and become a big wig
but for cryin out loud don't get burned.
Behind every good man is a good woman
so ladies toot your own horn,
They look for a diamond in the rough to change
starting back from the day he was born.
Sure there are many other little cliché sayings
I could include to enhance my list,
But I think you've heard enough of them
for you to catch on to my gist.
Maybe to you those are a drop in the bucket
and you'd like to hear a few more,
I'm sure they are just a stone's throw away
so that should be an easy chore.
Well, I guess it's back to the drawing board
out into the wild blue yonder,
I just wanted to pause and give you a break

because absence makes the heart grow fonder.
For cryin out loud get off your high horse
while you're down, get your ducks in a row,
Don't tuck your tail between your legs
tighten up and let's get on with the show.
I heard it through the grapevine, my friend,
good things come to those who wait,
But we're always putting the cart before the horse
in such a hurry to know our own fate.
Mark my words, the long and short of it
is opportunity never knocks twice,
Still, there's no use in cryin over spilled milk
for life is just a roll of the dice.
There's more than one way to skin a cat
once you learn this you may tend to brag,
You're not out of the woods, you're in hot water
if you let the cat out of the bag,
It goes without saying if you get in a pinch
figure out how to play your cards right,
Put the petal to the metal, put your best foot forward
and never give up without a fight.
It ain't over till the fat lady sings
for the record, I've never heard her song,
Let's set the record straight, you never say never
because she'll probably appear before long.
You won't know the difference a hundred years from now
but don't burn the candle at both ends,
The road to hell is paved with good intentions
for good intentions still turn into sins.

You're skating on thin ice and it's an uphill battle
if you rob Peter to pay Paul,
I'm not pulling your leg but you may beg to differ
it's your life and, my friend, that's your call.
You may think I've completely missed the boat
and I should just let sleeping dogs lie,
But still every dog has it's day
so don't give up till you give it a try.
There's a light at the end of the tunnel
so make hay while the sun still shines,
For we're all a hop, skip, and a jump away
from completely losing our minds.
Stop banging your head against a brick wall
when you can kill two birds with one stone,
The ball's in your court you'll be a basket case
if you try to live life all alone.
Cross that bridge when you come to it
just make sure you land on your feet,
When you're under the gun have something up your sleeve
else throw in the towel 'cause you're beat.
Don't try to keep up with the Joneses
you'll just stand out like a sore thumb,
I'm not trying to step on any ones toes
but, my friend, that sure seems kinda dumb.
I guess it takes one to know one
it's like the pot calling the kettle black,
I wouldn't touch that with a ten foot pole
'cause I'm pretty sure you ain't got my back.
Take a look at what the cat dragged in

don't bother worrying about where he's been,
he stays out till the cows come home
and returns three sheets to the wind.
Now I know you may not know me from Adam
and these sayings may drive you up the wall,
But go against the grain and take one for the team
it's a trip down memory lane for us all.
Really it's just the tip of the iceberg
so let's open up another can of worms,
If I'm going to land on my own two feet
I need to do it on my own terms.
I've still got a handful of old sayings
I can pull right off the top of my head,
When it rains it pours so let's go for broke
because this clichés parade still not dead.
What you see is what you get, my friend,
but things aren't always as they appear,
If you're up the creek without a paddle
better find a new way you can steer.
Just put one foot in front of the other
you can do it one step at a time,
A little birdie told me it's a foregone conclusion
half-baked ideas ain't worth a dime.
You'll get lost in the middle of nowhere
if you can't see the forest for the trees,
If you can't find your butt with both hands and a flashlight,
friend, its time you got down on your knees.
You can't teach an old dog new tricks
if things are coming apart at the seams,

Be careful because as fast as greased lightning
a U-turn can crush all your dreams.
Maybe you think I'm all talk and no action
or I'm just asleep at the wheel,
I can whip you with one arm tied behind my back
and it really wouldn't be a big deal.
Could be your thinking I don't have a clue
that I'm dumber than a box of rocks,
But even a blind squirrel finds an occasional acorn
so don't try to out-smart this ole fox.
It ain't rocket science, it all boils down to this,
it's never too late to learn,
So keep your chin up and your fingers crossed
hold your horses you'll soon get your turn.
You only live once and you can't take it with you
no doubt you can say that again,
You catch more flies with honey than vinegar
so I suggest you be sweet my ole friend.
This is where the rubber meets the road
where there's smoke there usually is fire,
It's there for the taking so go the extra mile
fight the good fight down to the wire.
That doesn't mean to fight like cats and dogs
instead you should fight like a man,
Fight fire with fire and figure it out
like they say do the best that you can.
You're just waiting for your ship to come in
and your bark is worse than your bite,
I hate to say this, but don't fear your own shadow

you'll be a sitting duck for a fight.
Life is short and you only live once
so dot your I's and cross your T's,
It goes without saying in the blink of an eye
life no longer seems like a breeze.
Take the path of least resistance I've heard
if not you may pay through the nose,
You might find you painted yourself in a corner
because you chose not to stay on your toes.
I suggest you get your head out of your butt
before the wool gets pulled over your head,
If you think I'm tryin to rub it in your face
give me the slip and choose your way instead.
One man's trash is another man's treasure
kinda rolls off the tip of your tongue,
You'd best discover old habits die hard
and create good habits while you are young.
You have nothing to fear but fear itself
and nothing succeeds like success,
Why one good turn deserves another,
my friend, that's anyone's guess.
My hands are tied my brain is fried
and my head is swimming around,
I'm making it by the skin of my teeth
still I never seem to make up much ground.
You may think I'm a few fries short of a happy meal
and, my friend, you could be right,
But just between you, me, and the bed post
I sure sleep awfully good every night.

Oops, sorry 'bout that, let's get back in the saddle
I went a barking up the wrong tree,
Just a fly in the ointment I lost sight of the big picture
for a second there I was talking about me.
Don't bite the hand that feeds you
don't be an old stick in the mud,
Don't look a gift horse in the mouth
or a cow when he's chewing his cud.
You'd agree life's not always a bed of roses
sometimes it's more like a labor of love,
We often get a taste of our own medicine
and have to look for some help from above.
The bigger they are the harder they fall
it's a dog eat dog world we live in,
All's well that ends well, so cool your jets
get your head in the game and you'll win.
Sometimes it feels like you can't win for losing
don't cut your nose off to spite your face,
For beauty is in the eye of the beholder
and this world is a drop dead gorgeous place.
Once again the blind is leading the blind
and you can bet the checks in the mail,
A bird in the hand is worth two in the bush
Don't jump the gun it's still too early to tell.
Now it may seem I'm all over the map
at least I'm willing to take a few shots,
I'm a jack-of-all-trades and master of none
and a leopard who can't change its spots.
Remember to always look at the bright side

its much better than taking a drug,
It's a no brainer and your ace in the hole
to make you feel snug as a bug in a rug.
Don't get all bent out of shape it don't help
it's not as if you lost an arm and a leg,
You may feel you're all dressed up with no place to go
but at least you're not so poor you must beg.
Women all say a good man is hard to find
they all want a feather in their cap,
A new lease on life or a wolf in sheep's clothing
is that sight for sore eyes just a trap.
It's as plain as the nose on your face
and now is as good a time as any,
A chain is only as strong as its weakest link
and, my friend, most chains have plenty.
Well I gave you some more oldies but goodies
I took my shot in the dark,
Honestly, it felt like it was all in a day's work,
nothing more than a walk in the park.
Sometimes I feel like a fish out of water
like I've jumped right out of the tank,
But not this time, I wrote a one-hit wonder
and, my friend, you can take that to the bank.

The Fireman

I watched as a big red fire truck
rushed upon the scene,
Men poured out from front and back,
they were big and tall and lean.
The home they were called to
was now totally engulfed in flames,
It only mattered what skills they had
no one cared about their names.
A little old lady was trapped inside
and a little baby too,
As the firemen stormed inside the home
the owner's tensions grew.
You see this family had nothing else
they had nowhere else to live,
If their home and loved ones could be saved
there's nothing this family wouldn't give.
Neither mom nor dad could fight through the fire
to save their little boy,
It was this baby boy and grandma too
who had brought them so much joy.
There was water flying in from everywhere
and chaos was in the air,
The seconds drug slowly by outside
for the frightened anxious pair.
Then suddenly through the smoke and flames
two charred firemen reappeared,
Their fireman clothes were torn and tattered
and they both had singed their beard.
It seemed as if a miracle had occurred

through the fire and smoky smell,
For in the fireman's arm was the baby boy
and they had grandma just as well.
The family now reunited rejoiced
as tears ran down their cheeks,
But they knew that life would be different
in the up and coming weeks.
Still, they were happy to be together again
though it came at quite a cost,
If not for two brave firemen that day
two precious lives would have been lost.
Grandma reached out for the brave fireman
and she asked him for his name,
She knew if not for this brave firefighter
she would have burnt up in those flames.
A tear welled up and ran down her cheek
as she hugged the massive man,
Now grandma proudly calls herself
this fireman's biggest fan.
As mom and dad held their baby boy
they both began to sob,
They realized despite danger to themselves
the firemen bravely did their job.
It takes a special person to be a fireman
they have a silent message they send,
They don't need to know your name
and they don't have to be your friend.
They just need to have an address
and know a life might be at stake,

Yes, you can count on a fireman to show up
and do whatever the job may take.

The Old Man and His Chair

At an old gas station on the edge of town
there was a very unusual site,
An old man sat in a rocking chair
he could be seen there day and night.
The old man never left his chair
he just rocked his life away,
he was famous to folks for miles around
for wise things he had to say.
Rain and sleet and snow could come
but the old man would never leave,
No one seemed to understand his purpose
or what he was trying to achieve.
One day the pastor from the local church
decided that he'd stop by,
he heard the old man wouldn't leave his chair
and he had always wondered why.
He pulled up and grabbed his Bible
and went over to where the old man sat,
he sat down in a chair next to him
and the two of them began to chat.
At first they talked about this and that
and the weather then the chair,
Then the preacher asked if he knew Jesus
and asked if he might say a prayer.
Stop right there the old man said
preacher you really do seem to care,
But no matter how much you pray for me
I ain't never gonna leave this chair.
The preacher man closed his Bible

and stood up from his chair real slow,
he said old man you can keep the chair
just let me pray before I go.
I never told you why I don't leave this chair
why I'm here all day and night,
But if you'd like to say a prayer for me
I guess that would be alright.
The preacher said a really nice prayer
he hoped would touch the old man's soul,
he wanted Jesus to come alive for him
for he knew he was mighty old.
When the prayer was done the man looked up
and with tears rolling from his eyes,
he told the preacher he was glad he'd prayed
and he could tell he was very wise.
But he said I'm a wise man too
at least I thought that was the case,
Yet, in all my wisdom and all my years
I never seemed to understand God's grace.
The preacher talked for quite a while longer
until he was sure the old man knew,
That even if he never left his chair
God would be sitting there with him too.
Then the preacher invited him to his home
for a hot meal, a shower, and a bed,
To his surprise the old man got up
and this is what the old man said.
Preacher man I've never left this chair
and I know you wonder why,

So, I'm gonna tell you 'cause you shared Jesus
and you actually made me cry.
I've never had anyone to love
I've had no children I've had no wife,
The only joy I've known was in this chair
sharing wisdom throughout my life.
Thousands of people have come to me
just to hear what I would say,
I never failed to share my wisdom
before I sent them on their way.
Yet, not one person ever asked about me
preacher you're the first to care,
So, you see the way I had it figured
I had no reason to leave my chair.
The preacher was touched and said
I know the words you speak are true,
God told me you needed a friend
the moment I sat down next to you.
The old man wasn't used to being out of his chair
he was finding it hard to stand,
Seeing his struggle the preacher reached out
and offered the old man his hand.
It soon turned into a warm embrace
and neither seemed to want to let go,
They finally did and the preacher noticed
the old man had a new glow.
Inspired, the preacher asked, how about it friend,
would you like a shower, a bed, and a meal?
The old man looked at his old rocking chair

and wisely said that sounds like a good deal.
The preacher knew the old man loved his chair
so he told him with a bit of luck,
he had room for him to ride in the cab
and room for his chair in the back of his truck.
Several years passed before the old man died,
and the preacher had him put in the ground,
But ever so often, he'd sit in that chair,
and pretend his old friend was still around.
Before the old man died they'd become best friends,
and the old man was thankful indeed,
he had met Jesus, and his life ended good,
because a preacher man planted a seed.

Trust and Obey

I had an unusual dream last night
the dream just blew me away,
In the dream God gave me a message
that He asked me to convey.
Some parts are a bit fuzzy
but the message was hard to hide,
God clearly said, whatever I needed,
He'd always be there to provide.
In the dream God gave me a check
worth a huge amount of money,
Maybe you don't believe in dreams,
and this story to you seems funny.
Yet, God had a special mission for me,
and I definitely had my doubts
For it wasn't exactly clear to me
what this mission was all about.
Still, God gave me a million dollars,
and I wasn't sure what to buy,
He told me to just trust Him,
and soon He would show me why.
What would I do with so much money,
my pocket was burning a hole
Would I keep it for God's mission
or would I be willing to sell my soul?
I heard the devil speak to me
then I heard God speak right back,
He warned me how ole satan
was trying to knock my life off track.
So, I said a little prayer to God

and ask Him to hold me tight,
I ask for help to ward off satan
so I could spend this money right.
Well, it wasn't long before a man
was standing at my door,
he was holding a box of items,
he said I'd need to do my chore.
I'm not sure where this man came from
all I know is he was nice,
he handed me the box he had
and said a million dollars was the price.
I handed him the check I had
then I took the box inside,
I could hardly wait to open it up
and see what things God would provide.
That much money for one small box
to me seemed a bit absurd,
But I quickly changed my mind
when I discovered God's Holy Word.
I'm sure most people find it crazy
to spend so much money this way,
It wasn't about the money, my friend,
it was about the message God wanted to convey.
See, God gave me all that money
for the money was obviously a must,
To see if I would purchase the box
and show Him how much I trust.
God had a mission for me
and He knew just what I'd need,

He gave me money to buy that box
so I could plant his seed.
You might have a different mission,
and it may have a different plot,
The important thing God wants to see
is you'll give Him all you've got.
It may seem a little funny to you
how God brings His will about,
The important thing God wants to see,
is you'll trust Him when you have doubt.
Yes, God gave me a dream,
with a message for me to convey,
He wants you to know He'll provide for you
if you'll totally trust Him and obey.

Two Crippled Friends

He had an unforgettable limp
I watched as he crossed the street,
Many times he had passed my house
and he's someone I wanted to meet.
I could never seem to find the courage
I wasn't quite sure what to say,
It looked like he desperately needed a friend
and I knew I must find a way.
One morning I noticed him passing by
he struggled as he took each step,
I still wasn't sure how to approach this man
yet, I knew he needed some help.
To tell the truth I was feeling some guilt
for not helping this man before,
I knew from hearing my neighbors talk
he had lost his leg in the war.
Today was the day so I walked across the yard
I greeted him and held out my hand,
he stood up straight and smiled at me
though it took all he had just to stand.
It didn't take me long to realize
what an incredible decision I'd made,
This man opened up and told me the story
how his leg was blown off by a grenade.
I invited him up and we sat on my porch
then I offered to make him some tea,
he smiled and graciously accepted my offer
and said he was enjoying his visit with me.
We talked for hours and he told me more stories

I didn't want our visit to end,
I realized though this man was crippled
I had just found an incredible friend.
He had lost his wife a few years ago
and his children had moved far away,
With no family around and only one leg
somehow he still embraced each new day.
As the weeks passed by our friendship grew
I was always there to give him a hand,
No longer did I see a man with a limp
Instead, I saw an incredibly strong man.
He still had a limp but he showed me his heart
and oh what a heart he had,
he always wore a smile no matter what happened
and he never got impatient or mad.
There was something different about my new friend
I'm not talking about the limp when he walked,
There was goodness and love in his actions
and there was kindness in the way he talked.
I'm not sure exactly what I did
that made my friend wonder about me,
But one day he boldly spoke up
and I saw something most folks never see.
I'll never forget that beautiful day,
sunlight from heaven glimmered through the trees,
there on my front porch a man with one leg
limped over then got down on his knees.
He lifted his head and looked me square in my eyes
and said friend I really do care,

Then he said if I didn't mind too much
he'd like to offer up a little prayer.
He said a prayer for me then he stood up
and limped to the bottom of my steps,
Stopping for a moment he looked back at me
and said, my friend, I hope this helps.
I watched as my friend limped across the yard
and I'll admit I felt a bit odd,
For I suddenly realized I was the cripple
who was living a life without God.
Those glimmers of sunlight had reached my porch
and one of them had just found my heart,
My cripple friend had introduced me to Jesus
and I now had a new friendship to start.
Yes, God can use anyone to show His love
as He did with my friend that day,
So, now I can boast of a home in heaven
because a crippled man showed me the way.

Section Six

RANDOM THOUGHTS

For Reflection:

Being a Christian is not a 24/7 prayer meeting. We have lots of fun along the way.

And also that every man should eat and drink, and enjoy the good of all his labour, it is the gift of God.

—Ecclesiastes 3:13

Random Thoughts

Alienation

I'll be the first to admit I'm dumb
when it comes to talking outer space,
I don't know what all is out there
I just know it's a mighty big place.
I'm not just talking about things we daily see
ordinary objects if you get my gist,
I'm talking about flying UFOs
and the claims that aliens exist.
Maybe they do, and maybe they don't
I haven't seen the latest Vegas odds,
I wouldn't even give it a second thought
except they now claim aliens are gods.
They claim aliens are darting around so fast
that they're impossible for us to capture,
And Christians won't ascend to heaven;
one day they'll be sucked up in an alien rapture.
My friend, you may think I'm playing a joke
but this is truly some Hollywood scheme,
It's obvious from the agenda they're pushing
that they don't play on Jesus's team.
They are just entertaining us you say
but I contend the goal is to indoctrinate,
Between Washington, Disney, and Hollywood,
my friend, I pray it's not too late.
We have plenty of other problems on earth
we sure don't need to worry about Mars,
While the films may be entertaining
we're being brainwashed by these so-called stars.
Like I said, I can be quite dumb,

as to whether aliens are fake or they're real,
But listen up close, and don't miss this truth
because, my friend, the truth's a big deal.
I don't want you to miss the real rapture
thinking aliens will beam your soul up one day,
God's Word can be trusted and it clearly says
Jesus is the truth, the life, and the way.
Enjoy yourself as you watch Hollywood shows
but don't buy into their little Martian tales,
If you do, you'll miss the rapture to heaven,
and you'll catch a UFO spaceship to hell.

Back in the Day

Back in the day when I was young
I used to play some ball,
As time passed by my body aged
until I couldn't play at all.
I guess I shouldn't complain
after all the fun I had,
Still, I miss the game and competing
and it makes me kinda sad.
Standing in centerfield
at the base of the outfield wall,
I could throw a strike to home plate
without touching the ground at all.
I was also an awesome pitcher
I loved striking batters out,
Just me against the other guy,
that's what pitching was all about.
I could hit long home runs
batting from both sides of the plate,
I was an All-American at a young age,
it seemed baseball was my fate.
As the story unfolded and time drug on
it didn't turn out that way,
I'm still not sure why I did some things
I did back in the day.
But God knows best, He has a plan,
that's all I need to know,
Still, I wonder with the talent I had
could I have made it to "The Show."
Those days are all behind me now

they produced a lot of fun,
It's safe to say I have good memories,
I've had my day in the sun.
There are times I reminisce
about the days when I played ball,
But I realize that wasn't my fate
my life had a different call.
Back in the day I never dreamed
I would become a railroad man,
That's okay I'm good with that
that obviously was God's plan.
There's a million players or more
who are now way past their prime,
Their memories from back in the day
will surface from time to time.
I hope they're like me when this occurs
and it brings a smile to their face,
and they realize the man they are today
is because of God's amazing grace.

Christmas Reality

Love and laughter are everywhere, it's the spirit of the
Christmas season,
Though there's presents all around the tree, we each still know
the real reason.
We all come together as family, to enjoy the holiday fun,
But, we're here to celebrate Jesus, the birth of God's
heavenly Son.
Over time we've changed some things, and created our own
traditions,
Still, we should take great care, and not forget the beginning
conditions.
God left us a beautiful story, from two thousand and some
years ago,
Of how He gave us a Savior, so we each would definitely know.
Christ is at the beginning of Christmas, and the
M-A-S at the end,
Is to remind us God's heavenly Son, is the one who
mastered-all-sin.
From the beginning like the wise men, who gave gold,
frankincense, and myrrh,
We saw the importance of giving gifts, and it helped our
tradition occur.
I don't think Christ minds, that we give gifts as we celebrate
His birth,
If we remember it's not the gifts, allowing Christmas to have its
true worth.

It's a time of joy and laughter, and giving gifts to the
ones we love,
Never forget there'd be no Christmas, without our gift from
God up above.

Coffee

I'm just not a morning person
guess that's always been the case,
Until I've had my morning coffee
you'd be wise to give me space.
Give me a shot or two of caffeine
I'm out the door and on my way,
Now that I've had my morning coffee
I'm prepared to face the day.
If I'm still a little cranky
by the time I get to work,
I'll pour me another cup
To keep from acting like a jerk.
By the middle of the morning
when I go to check the mail,
I sneak down to the break room
I am drawn there by the smell.
I find the break room empty,
but the coffee isn't hot,
So, I take it upon myself
to close the door and brew a pot.
It seems my morning cup of Joe
has worn off much too soon,
I need to freshen up myself
so I can make it until noon.
There's a chance I may be wrong
I'm just working off a hunch,
But I may have time for a Starbucks
when I leave to grab some lunch.
One more cup leaving work

as I'm walking out the door,
Maybe I can make it to the house
without stopping by the store.
I really love my coffee
and I'm not ashamed to say,
It's the way I start every morning
and it's how I end each day.
I truly am addicted, I
guess I'll drink coffee till I'm dead,
Heck I brew me up a fresh pot
right before I go to bed.
I could probably do without my coffee
but I don't intend to try,
If you're a coffee drinker, my friend,
you probably understand just why.
Coffee helps get you going
and it gets you through your day,
If you can't get a cup of coffee
there's a price that people pay.
You are one of millions of people
who need coffee to start each morning,
Until you get a cup or two
your prone to pounce without a warning.
If you don't get your morning Joe
it becomes a really big deal,
My friend, I totally get it,
I know exactly how you feel.
So brew up a nice fresh pot
and have yourself a cup or two,

Don't get around any other people
or go to work until you do.
If I see you out at the office,
or at Starbucks on the fly,
We can grab a cup together
and, my friend, I'll even buy

Country Boy

I'll always be a country boy
I'm country to the bone,
I was country as a little boy
I'm country now that I'm grown.
Some people call me a redneck,
but that's simply not the case,
If you think I'm redneck because I'm country
then, my friend, your way off base.
Country is a kind of living
that has a way that's all its own,
You learn to entertain yourself outside
instead of playing on your phone.
Swinging on vines, throwing rocks in the pond
or going hunting to kill a rabbit,
Driving a tractor and working in the garden
just becomes a country boy's habit.
Catching lighting bugs, catching fish
you might even catch a snake,
Milking cows and baling hay
going skinny dippin in the lake.
Chasing bumble bees, building a fort
or squirting each other with a hose,
If it's working hard or how to have fun,
you can bet a country boy knows.
I'm country strong I can work all day
and still go out on the town at night,
But, I won't act like some redneck,
and go to town just looking to fight.
I'm not trying to hate on rednecks

I'm just claiming that country is cool,
It's a country boy who'll mind his manners
while a redneck's acting a fool.
I love the life of a country boy
I love being around country folks, too;
heck, I learned how to be a country boy
watching what other country folks do.
I'll always be a country boy
I'm as country as I can be,
You may take me out of the country
but you'll never take the country out of me.

Elevate Yourself

Why do people feel the need, to cut each other down,
Since day one, it seems this human trait has been around.
It doesn't make sense, but still I know it's true,
People can't stand to see others, excel at what they do.
You know what I mean, so listen up, don't play dumb and deaf,
At times you've done this very thing, to feel better
about yourself.
It never really does you good, to thwart someone's success.
Trying to elevate yourself, usually just makes a mess.
It doesn't change what you've done, or who you really are,
The only thing it really does is leave a nasty scar.
Wouldn't it be better to compliment, and help your fellow man,
Instead of trying to bring him down, lend him a helping hand.
Finding good in people you meet, is truly the way to go,
For the way to elevate yourself, is by helping others grow.
Remember when others succeed, and put a trophy upon
their shelf,
You don't need to bring them down, to feel better
about yourself.

Encouragement

Regardless of where I may travel
no matter what city or state I'm in,
I see people who need encouragement
as they struggle to conquer their sin.
We face a lot of challenges these days
it can certainly get you down,
So, I share the love of Jesus
and a smile to replace their frown.
Sometimes a word of encouragement
can go a mighty long way,
You may cause someone's spirits to lift
and help them make it through their day.
I've seen it happen many times
you never know who you'll touch,
The good news for you, my friend,
is encouragement won't cost you much.
It don't take much, just a little time
to say an encouraging word or two
You'll be amazed at the results you'll get
and what an encouraging word can do.
I'm sure as you've lived your life
you've been able to discover,
Encouragement can lift the spirits
when it comes from the heart of another.
It matters not how young or how old
what gender or race you are,
Everyone in every city and state
is dealing with some kind of scar.
So, give the gift of encouragement

to your friends, family, and peers,
Trust that it won't go unnoticed
and will seldom fall on deaf ears.
Still, you may not be sold on encouragement
you don't think people need it to get by,
I would encourage you not to discard it,
at least not until you give it a try.

Fate

There are things in our lives that happen to us each,
We try to take control, but it's just not in our reach.
Are our lives mapped out, there's still quite some debate,
It's the age-old belief, we all know as fate.
Try as we may, to work out our own plans,
There's nothing we can do when it lies in God's hands.
Not all folks believe in this thing we call fate,
They believe it's up to them and the choices they make.
Still, others believe no matter what path they take,
Life is predetermined, and nothing is at stake.
Friend, you only live once, and there's no room for doubt,
So, open up God's Word, and you'll figure this question out.
The fate of your soul, God leaves up to you,
Yes, we each have a choice to decide what to do.
Since our personal choice matters in something so great,
Don't get lured in by this thing we call fate.
Fate is just a feeling, of how you think things will be,
The choices of your free will are really life's key.
God has a purpose, and He always has a plan,
It's true, He still holds the whole world in His hands.
We all still have decisions, some small and some great,
And the paths we choose, help God determine our fate.

Guitar Blues

I've watched people play the guitar
and I'll admit it was really a treat,
But I tried it myself and it didn't work out,
it sounded like I was playin' with my feet.
I watched them flyin' up and down the scales
making music that sounded so sweet,
So I grabbed my guitar and tried it again
it still sounded like I was playin' with my feet.
When other people play it's like breathin' in air,
the pickin' and strummin' they do,
When I try it sounds like I'm playin' with my feet
and I get discouraged and blue.
There are thousands of people who play the guitar
they keep such an awesome beat,
I don't understand why when I try it myself
it sounds like I'm playing with my feet.
Yes, there are some truly amazing guitarists;
you see them playin' on the corner of the street.
But no, not me, when I give it a try,
it still sounds like I'm playin' with my feet.
Let's put things into a proper perspective
these guys practice for hours on end,
It's like they are married to their guitar
or at least it becomes their best friend.
They practice so long they break their strings
and calluses appear on their hands,
They play until their fingers are bleeding
for all that practice, I'm not a big fan.
Maybe that helps explain it, my friend,

for I just keep tryin' to cheat,
I never put time into practicing my guitar
that's why it sounds like I'm playin' with my feet.
Those guys are incredible I'll have to admit
to play like them would be really neat,
Still, I'm not gonna practice, so I guess it's a fact
I'll always sound like I'm playin' with my feet.

Guns

Where did you get that ammo
why do you have that gun,
Do you intend to break the law
or are you just having fun.
Are you going to hunt for Bambi
or shoot targets at the range,
Maybe you'll become a serial killer
or something else that's strange.
I guess we never really know
how a gun's going to be used,
It is always up to the owner
whether or not the gun's abused.
Whether you live in the big city
or in the country on a farm,
Sooner or later you'll need a gun
to protect your family from harm.
The evil that a gun protects us from
is the evil that abuses the gun,
It's not always easy to identify evil
until after the damage is done.
It's not the guns that are evil
we'd be foolish to take guns away,
For the evil will always keep their guns
no matter what our laws might say.
So maybe you're just protecting yourself
or hunting to kill you some meat,
Maybe your planning nothing but evil
gunning down people in the street.
Either way rest assured, it's not the gun

that is evil and breaking the law,
It's the human brain and the human heart
that is broken and has the flaw.

Habits

I have a little bad habit
I bet you've got one too,
The more I chose to feed my habit
the more my habit grew.
I didn't like my habit
so I decided to put it down,
No matter how hard I tried
it still followed me around.
This is not my only habit
I'm afraid it has some friends,
While most of them are good,
some of them are flat out sins.
Sometimes the water I wade in
gets awfully dark and deep,
I know I'll never change my habits
unless I change the company I keep.
We acquire both good and bad habits
as we endeavor along our way,
The habits that we have tomorrow
are our choices from today.
It's true we'll never rid ourselves
of these bad habits known as sin,
But reading the Bible and praying to God
would be a good place to begin.
Here's another tip for you, my friend,
if you've got bad habits to lose,
Pay a little bit more attention
to the company that you choose.
Who you spend your time with

is a very important step,
So, surround yourself with Godly people
and ask God for daily help.
Jesus is the "Good Shepherd"
and He knows the company we keep,
Yet, He's always there to lend a hand,
and help protect His flock of sheep.
Be careful to keep good company
for it makes a difference indeed,
Always look to God for help
whenever you feel you have a need.
I share this information, my friend,
yet, it's my habits I must fight,
It's not your habits I'll answer for
when I'm standing in God's sight.
But, if you're like me, my friend,
you've got some bad habits too,
And the habits of the company you keep
are rubbing off on you.
Remember it is God himself
who protects and guides His sheep,
Still, it's up to you to do your part,
and pay attention to the company you keep.

Instant Gratification

You've got to have it now
you're not sure if you can wait,
It too hard to have patience
you just want to know your fate.
You want a pretty diamond
and not some lump of coal,
There's no need to dirty your hands
trying to ascertain your goal.
Just give you what you want
and give it to you now,
You don't need to hear the details
and no one needs to tell you how.
Is this the way you live, my friend,
like you're on a constant life vacation,
The only thing you seem to know
is instant gratification.
You feel you should have everything
your little heart desires,
Everyone around you is miserable
always putting out your fires.
If this is how you live your life
because you never learned to wait,
Listen to my advice, my friend,
before you find it's too late.
Patience is a virtue
and it's part of God's big plan,
Everyone has to learn to wait
although you don't think you can.
You want instant gratification,

it's the only thing you know,
But, God wants to teach you patience,
that's the only way you will grow.
You need to learn patience, my friend,
and you need to learn it now,
God will give you all the details
and He'll even show you how.
I hope you don't ignore these words
it's important for you to see,
Instantly getting everything you want
is not how God intended life to be.
God wants you to learn to trust Him
and stop worrying about your fate,
Instant gratification's not the answer,
for good things come to those who wait.

It's a Small World

I went to the store, I went to the mall
I went to a town far away,
No matter how far from home I'd roam
the same thing always came into play.
It's one thing to meet people you know
at the store just down the street,
But, roam far away from your home,
and those people you're not expecting to meet.
There are towns, cities, and millions of people
but, I'll tell you this one thing, my friend,
Sometimes the connections we make with people
remind us what a small world we're in.
Maybe it's a neighbor, a teammate, or an old boss
or just someone you met at the zoo,
You find yourself a long way from home
but, somehow that person somehow knows you.
I dare not say how it occurs this way
for it happens to both a boy and a girl,
I'm not a fan for things I don't understand
I only know it's a mighty small world.
People I know, know people I know
And somehow they all become friends,
One by one and little by little
it becomes a small world we live in.
Believe it or not, this is nothing new
This is always the way it has been,
You'll meet these people wherever you go
and realize what a small world we're in.
Don't take my word, check it out for yourself

when you travel to a land far away,
I bet you'll find out I'm telling the truth
and these are the words you'll hear people say.
O wow, I knew you mom or your dad,
your coach or your last girlfriend,
You'll remember this poem, and think to yourself
it really is a small world we live in.

Kin Folk

It really is a special time
when loved ones gather around,
A group of kin folk we call family
where a special love is found.
Our crazy busy paths don't cross
as often as they should,
But, love's kept alive in each of our hearts
and we mean one another good.
Yes, family is a special bond you have
for those who are your kin,
You keep that love alive in your heart
till you can see them once again.
Ever so often you slow life down
and all come together for a day,
To enjoy being around the ones you love
and hearing things that kin folk say.
"How've you been", "let me hug your neck",
"it's good to see your beautiful smile,
We laugh and share as if we daily meet
though we all know it's been quite a while.
There is always good food and stories are shared
from memories we all recall,
It's a special day when we get back together
and a good time is had by all.
As is always the case when enjoying yourself
the time flies by so fast,
Though we must depart we all seem to cherish
the bonds we have from our past.
We go separate ways but we each have new memories

we'll carry from all of our kin,
They will be the stories we share with each other
when we get back together again.
So, remember to be thankful for all your kin folk,
God so graciously put in your life,
For family is more than brothers and sisters
and a husband and his wife.
You may think family only lives in your home
but you still have a whole family tree,
So, once in a while just slow down your life,
then your kin folk you'll have time to see.

Nature Walk

There's nothing like a nature walk
to bring solace to your soul,
A perfect way to restore some peace
that the devil might have stole
There's something about God's creation
and the solitude of being alone,
No busy sounds from city life
no distractions from your phone.
You may bring along hiking boots
or perhaps your fishing rod,
But its' mostly about the scenery
and the time you spend with God.
Just take a moment to sit and relax
in the quietness of the shade,
It won't take long to get awestruck
from the beauty God has made.
Then step into the sunlight
and watch the colors dance around,
Nowhere else but God's creation
can these wondrous things be found
There's no way to properly convey
the beauty that nature can bring,
It's an experience like no other
when nature's sounds begin to sing.
Your senses start to come to life
from all the sights and sound,
No doubt when God created nature
He created hallowed ground.
I know words can't bring alive

the magical things nature can do,
I suggest you try it for yourself
and see what nature does for you.
God put together the wonders of nature
in a most extraordinary way,
Yet they often go unnoticed
as we go through our normal day.
So, I suggest you take a nature walk
and leaves all your worries behind,
Grab your hiking boots and fishing rod
you'll be pleased with what you find.
It should come as no surprise, my friend,
for God always has a reason,
He wants you to enjoy your nature walk
regardless of the season.
God created a world of things
and some of them seem odd,
But, I'm convinced He created nature
to display the awesomeness of God.

Pendulum of Life

Without the day there is no night,
without a wrong there is no right.
Without a girl there would be no boy,
without sorrow we'd feel no joy.
Without a gain there could be no loss,
there is no hope without the cross.
Without legs you'd have no feet,
without blood your heart can't beat.
Without eyes you could never see,
without your birth you'd never be.
Without fatigue you never need rest,
without God you'll never be blessed.
Without ears you'd hear no sound,
without salvation for hell your bound.
Without smell you'd have no taste,
without abundance we'd have no waste.
Without heaven there would be no earth,
only thru Jesus can you find your worth.
Without a this there is no that,
without a head you'd need no hat.
Without children you have no mother,
you can't have one without the other.
Without a galaxy there are no stars,
without sin Christ would have no scars.
Without the truth there could be no lie,
without tears you would never cry.
Without clouds there is no rain,
without feelings you have no pain.
If it is free there is no cost,

without the blood of Jesus, you'd be lost.
Without love there would be no hate,
without time you'd never be late.
Without life there would be no death,
without oxygen you'd never catch your breath.
Without a beginning there is no end,
without temptation there is no sin.
There's a beginning and end to every day,
Jesus is the truth, the life, the way.
Every mountain top has its peak,
God is strong when you are weak.
The sun will rise and it will set,
it's hard to remember what you forget.
You see, my friend, it really is true,
there's always two sides for you to view.
The pendulum always swings and sways,
giving us perspective from both ways.
Follow the pendulum from side to side,
take a closer look before you decide.
Do you see the world from a limited view,
because the pendulum never swings back to you.
It matters not if you're a father or mother,
you're usually stuck on one side or the other.
Open your eyes and open your mind,
you may be surprised at what you find.
Nothing ventured then nothing is gained,
and nothing grows without the rain.
The same is true if you feed your pride,
for you'll never see the other side.

You'll be stuck with a limited view,
until the pendulum of life runs over you.

Resolution Roulette

Another year is almost over
and a new one lingers near,
You debate what you'll give up first
will it be smoking or drinking beer.
You'd also like to lose a few pounds
or maybe fix up the ole lake house,
But you haven't kept last year's resolution
of spending more time with your spouse.
It seems the new year is a time for many
where resolutions are boldly made,
Yet, the question is how long before we'll bail,
once our resolution plans are laid.
It's really a voluntary thing we do
no one's there to twist our wrist,
I'm sure every single one of us
have good intentions when making our list.
But, it's not long before the ordinary person
has thrown that list away,
The lofty goals of our new year's list
have somehow just gone astray.
It's true old habits don't die easy
and new habits are hard to create,
Yet when the new year rolls around again
we seem to always take the same bait.
This year you're going to eat better food
and pay more attention to your health,
Or maybe you're going to find a better job
to create more family wealth.
Perhaps you aim to have a better home life

or maybe take more family trips,
Still, it's not long before the hands of habit
has you firmly back in its grip.
Cheer up, my friend, we all get caught
in this new year resolution trap,
Its true change is hard for everyone
it never just falls in our lap.
But never give up there's always hope
keep setting your goals lofty and high,
If you failed at last year's resolutions
thank God for a new year to try.

Rock Jock

Maybe all you see when you look at me
is just some stupid jock,
But I was smart enough, my friend,
to build my house upon the rock.
I probably spend too much time
trying to win some silly game,
Still, I'm sharing Jesus along my way
and in that I find no shame.
There's a lot of blood, sweat, and tears
shed by people playing sports,
Watch their habits long enough
and they are sure to show their warts.
It's a perfect breeding ground
to set a Christian example that's right,
I may be just some stupid jock
but I can be both salt and light.
As always there will be people
who make fun of me and mock,
But the battle I'll win, I won't give in,
for Jesus is my rock.
Whether you're playing the game of life
or you're playing some game of sports,
Without the rock of Jesus by your side
your game will seem out of sorts.
I'm not throwing up some "Hail Mary"
so you've got a chance to win the game,
I'm offering a chance to play with the MVP
and Jesus is His name.
Life is over in a blink, my friend,

216

and time's ticking off your clock,
So don't delay, say yes today
and let Jesus be your rock.
Maybe you think I'm some stupid jock
and that's all I'll ever be,
But, when life's game is over, I'll go to heaven
because the rock is inside of me.

Second Chances

Into every life a little rain must fall, we each have a
spot reserved,
We seldom get a second chance, but I believe it's well deserved.
Which of us and even you, has not a mistake been made,
In a moment, not thinking clear, a high price must be paid.
The end for some, the beginning for others, when from
someone's kind heart,
A second chance was handed out, giving life a brand new start.
Some believe a second chance for others should not exist,
Instead there should be a consequence, for choosing to
take a risk.
I agree with a wrong choice, one should pay some kind of price,
Yet, a second chance upon completion, I think would be
quite nice.
Although it was long ago, Christ hung upon a cross,
To allow us a second chance, and to us there was no cost.
Christ can do what man cannot, He used this example to teach,
While we all fail at times, a second chance is deserved by each.
There are consequences for wrong actions we may choose,
While accountable, my friend, a second chance you do not lose.
If you can give a second chance, but you're not sure what to do,
Think of Christ on the cross, and remember what He has
done for you.

Sunshine

I watch as the sun appears
and moves across the morning sky,
I take another sip of coffee
and let out my usual sigh.
There's nothing more spectacular
than a view of the morning sun,
Unless perhaps it's a sunset
to signify the day is done.
From horizon to horizon
I stand and watch in awe,
Beauty stretching from East to West
without a single flaw.
A beautiful picture to start my day
as I watch a new sunrise,
What the Master will create today
has become my morning prize.
Then my day ends with another scene
one too awesome to forget,
The same beauty that started my day,
I now see in God's sunset.
Its' a blessing to see them both
I'd hate to have to pick just one,
God does some of His best work
with the rise and setting of the sun.
God has a purpose for everything,
like how He starts and ends each day.
I'm not exactly sure what His purpose is
but I'm sure thankful for His display.

Thanksgiving

Its' a special day of food and fun, we fondly call Thanksgiving
If your family don't enjoy this holiday, you're simply just
not living.
As you shovel in another bite of turkey and some dressing,
Be reminded of the many ways our God keeps on blessing.
Moments earlier a prayer was said, while everyone's head
was bowed,
Giving thanks for blessings throughout the year, a loving
God allowed.
Though some swear this special day was put aside for eating,
Friend you've missed the point, if you're not thankful while
you're meeting.
Children are playing everywhere, and smiles are all around,
Each different loved one you see, there's a memory to be found.
There's aunts and uncles, nieces, and nephews, even sisters
and brothers,
granddads and grandmoms, sons, and daughters, and lots of
dads and mothers.
Don't get caught up in the food, and allow that to be
your measure,
Remember the people you gather with, are what your heart
should treasure.
There are many other reasons we should show our gratitude,
But as long as you give God thanks, it's okay to enjoy the food.
Don't forget throughout the year, the things God
helped you face.
Know you're here and blessed today, because of God's
abundant grace.

Of all the holidays we observe, I'm not sure where this
one ranks,
But, we shouldn't need a special day to remember to give
God thanks.

The Bottom Line

Please spare me all the details
I think I'll get by just fine,
If you don't mind get to the point
and give me the bottom line.
I like to hear the particulars
and I want to know the plan,
But not if it takes half the day
just so I can understand.
Now it may come back to bite me
it may even put me in a bind,
Still, it's better than gathering details
that do nothing but clutter my mind.
I know most people like details
and I can certainly understand why,
Still, I say keep them to yourself
I'll manage to somehow get by.
They say there's dollars in the details
if you'll just take the time,
I've got better things to do, my friend,
please, just give me the bottom line.
You may think details are the bomb
and you don't think this poem is funny,
You may even think I'm stupid
for not taking time to make more money.
Maybe you think it makes no sense
not getting all the details you can,
You think dealing with someone like me
is way too hard to understand.
I tell you, friend, it makes good sense

to someone who thinks like me,
I don't have half a day for details
I've got other places to be.
All that money you think I'm missing
from my bottom line,
All that money belongs to God
that money's not even mine.
I have a philosophy I've lived by,
it has aged just like a fine wine,
I let God deal with the details
I just focus on the bottom line.
That way details don't bog me down
they're not cluttering up my brain,
When I focus on the bottom line,
it helps to keep this ole boy sane.
My friend, you may want your details
I get it, that's totally fine,
When it comes to dealing with this ole boy
please, just stick to the bottom line.

The Game of Life

Everybody wants to be a winner
that's why you play the game,
Yet, when you give it all you've got,
the loser should feel no shame.
It's true no one likes a sore loser
so you must learn to accept defeat,
Whether you win or lose the game,
what's most important is how you compete.
For every game has a winner
and of course a loser as well,
The way you handle each outcome
leaves behind a story to tell.
The winner is always happy
but if he's cocky and arrogant with pride,
Although he may be labeled the winner
he gains no respect from the losing side.
A real winner can have jubilation
without rubbing it in his opponents face,
There's something to be said for a winner
who can do it with dignity and grace.
It's equally important for the losers
when their team goes down in defeat,
To hold up their head and credit the winners
and admit they just got beat.
You don't have to be happy about losing
but you should give the winners their due,
Then next time your team comes out on top
the same respect will come back to you.
That's the ideal way it should happen

but that's not how it always turns out,
Still, learning how, to win and how to lose,
is a big part of what sports is about.
The same is true in life, my friend,
although it's not a game with a ball,
We learn to be grateful when things go our way
and how to get back up when we fall.
It's good to have dignity and grace in success
and keep your head high when facing defeat,
It's how you should play the game of life
no matter what opposition you meet.
You may be at the top or the bottom of the heap
for in life you never know what to expect,
Still, remember your leaving a story behind
leave behind one that will earn you respect.
So whether you're playing a game with a ball
or it's the game of life that you're in,
Don't forget its most important how you treat others,
not whether you lose or win.

The Greatness of Golf

There's something about a round of golf
that brings solace to my soul,
Although when I decide to tee it up,
that's usually not my goal.
I started playing the game of golf
as just a teenage boy,
To smack that ball and watch it fly
just filled my heart with joy.
Just me against the course, you see,
that's how I played the game,
If I didn't measure up,
I had no one else to blame.
I am a very competitive person,
I've always played to win,
No matter where I tee it up,
the course is not my friend.
Now the course is not my enemy
I wouldn't go quite that far,
Still, I'm not there to befriend the course
I'm there to conquer "Old Man Par".
I'm not sure just how it happens
but as each round starts to unfold,
The peace I feel as I walk the course
starts to creep inside my soul.
Don't get me wrong I'm still at war
and I aim to pass the test,
Yet while I battle to conquer the course
I feel my soul's at perfect rest.
It seems bizarre yet still it's true

both things can coexist,
Somehow, I remain at peace with the course
without putting my game at risk.
It's the beauty of the game of golf
that makes this challenge so grand,
If you've never teed it up, my friend,
you'll never fully understand.
All I know is many years ago
I got hooked on the game of golf,
My competitive fire's come to life
every single time I tee off.
Somehow as the years have passed by,
the course has consumed my soul,
And the beauty of peace and competitive fire
is a story that can't go untold.

Tough Love

Back when I was a young man
a long long time ago,
My decisions weren't always the best
and my standards were really quite low.
I knew there would be consequences
when stupid things were done,
Yet, that didn't seem to slow me down,
I was too busy having fun.
I certainly knew right from wrong
yes my parents saw to that,
Despite all their parental guidance
I still acted like a brat.
I also did some good things
to help balance out the scale,
Still, I mostly did whatever I wanted,
and I gave my parents hell.
Well as you might imagine
this wasn't ok with mom and pop,
So, they put together a little plan
to bring my defiance to a stop.
A lot of discipline and a lot of love
was the plan they put in play,
Their masterful plan worked like a charm
and made me the man I am today.
Spare the rod and spoil the child
is clearly what the Bible states,
Mix that with some good ole fashion love
and a good child it creates.
Back then it was called tough love

and it's how most children were raised,
When you did wrong, you got a whipping,
if you did right, then you were praised.
It's really a simple little concept
that parents have lost along the way,
The rod is spared and the child is spoiled
in most homes we see today.
I'm thankful I was raised on tough love
and my parents didn't spare the rod,
I'm grateful I had parents
who taught me to love and honor God.
I hope and pray more parents realize
tough love is the way to go,
So the children of this new generation
can continue to flourish and grow.
The only way this can ever happen
is for parents to look to God above,
Stop sparring the rod and spoiling the child
and give them some good ole fashion tough love.

Wedding Vows

What a special day for a man and wife when they exchange
vows of love.
It's amazing how vows can change when push comes to shove.
Why is it we say these vows on our wedding day,
if when our life has hardships, they are only words we say.
At first life feels grand, and we share common dreams,
nothing can tear us apart, or at least that's how it seems.
Then somewhere along the way, we learn those other things,
that change how we view our vows, because of the hardship
it brings.
We only want "for better," the "for worse" is out the door.
When commitment takes effort, we don't want it anymore.
"In sickness" we can't deal with, it's only health we will embrace.
If life takes a sudden turn, we find someone to take their place.
It's easy for people to say words, that give marriage its start,
But man and wife must commit to vows, or it soon will
fall apart.
Life gets hard, I will admit, but we must somehow find a way,
To remember the vows we take, are more than just
words we say.

Section Seven

GOD THE FATHER – GOD THE SON

For Reflection:

A more sacred Father and Son relationship can't be found and, we are the beneficiary of Gods perfect plan.

For God so loved the world, that He gave His only begotten Son, that whosoever believeth in Him should not perish, but have everlasting life. For God sent not His Son into the world to condemn the world; but that the world through Him might be saved.

—John 3:16-17

God the Father – God the Son

Boss Man

Jesus tell me where I should go
although I don't really want a boss,
I'll follow where ever you lead, Lord
For you died upon that cross.
I can't imagine how you felt
dealing with such pain,
Yet, it was the Father's will
to wash away sin's awful stain.
Since you died such a cruel death
to set this captive free,
I can help the hurting needy people
you daily put in front of me.
You've been so good to me, oh Lord,
it's truly a blessed life I live,
Show me which people need your love
and help my heart be willing to give.
I'll be obedient and listen Lord
I'll do what you tell me to do,
I'm only your broken vessel
but, I want to live my life for you.
Mold me, make me, show me, Lord,
with every step I take,
There's a lost and dying world out there
I know exactly what's at stake.
I don't mind you being my boss
that's just my silly human pride,
I'll go anywhere the pathway leads
I know you're always by my side.
Since you died such a painful, cruel death

just to save me from my sin,
The least I can do is take up my cross
and go out and fish for men.
I'm willing for you to be my boss
I'll go wherever I am told,
I want to share the love of Jesus
and help bring sinners into your fold.
The blood you shed upon that cross
is far more than I 'll ever deserve,
So, tell me Lord where I should go
and I'll gladly go out and serve.

Captain Jesus

Do you ever feel it's all you can do
just to keep your life afloat,
What you need is a helping hand
from Captain Jesus to guide your boat.
Your being tossed both to and fro
by life's storm and it's mighty wind,
You need mercy and forgiveness
for all those times you've sinned.
You grab the stern and pull and tug
you set your mast up high,
But, you can't find peaceful waters
no matter how hard you try.
You pulled up anchor to escape the storm
but, the storm blew you away,
Never once while you fought the storm
did you take time to stop and pray.
I know your not a child anymore
and you think now that your grown,
You can face whatever life throws your way
and you can face those storms alone.
I'm sure you've faced a storm or two
so, now you may tend to gloat,
But the storms of life will soon win out
without Captain Jesus in your boat.
Yes, you will need a helping hand,
one that's strong and true,
You need Jesus to guide your boat and tell you exactly
what to do.
No matter how much experience you have,

or the size of the boat you're in,
You'll never keep your heart afloat
while you're drowning in all your sin.
Its best to give your life to Jesus
and leave it in the hands of the potter,
That's where you'll find God's forgiveness
and how you'll find some peaceful water.
Captain Jesus is there when you're lost
to lend His helping hand,
He'll calm whatever storms you face
and steer your boat onto dry land.
Once Jesus leads your ship ashore
and your back on solid ground,
You'll look for Captain Jesus's help
every time a storm cloud rolls around.

Cling to the Cross

The devil tugs and pulls at me,
he wants to see me trip.
I'm clinging to the cross of Christ
I dare not lose my grip.
No matter how hard satan tempts
or the storms of life may blow,
I'm clinging to the cross of Christ
it's the only safe place I know.
I may lose a loved one or a friend
I'm still clinging to the cross,
Jesus is the only one I can trust
to give me peace with such a loss.
Lose my car, or lose my job,
I may even lose my home,
I'm still clinging to the cross
Lord, help my heart not to roam.
Even when satan puts me in a bind
no matter how I turn and toss,
I know my anchor holds in Jesus
so I'm clinging to the cross.
You have a choice, just like me
that's the point I want to get across,
In the storms of life, cling to Jesus
and to the promise of the cross.

Connect the Dots

Are you trying to figure out your life
but there's too many twisted plots,
Everything seems to swirl around
and you can't connect the dots.
Problems fly in from everywhere
to fill your day with pain,
You don't have time to solve them
your busy just trying to stay sane.
My friend, you're one of millions of people
who wake up to this problem each day,
They're searching for some magical spell
or some fancy words to say.
Problems are just a part of life
unfortunately, they'll always exist,
Still, you need to devise a plan
to exercise when your problems persist.
I don't suggest you tackle this task
by relying on just yourself,
You need God and He'll do no good
if you put Him on a shelf.
You can try to connect the dots
as they swirl around in your head,
But, I suggest you lean on God
and ask Him for help instead.
If you're not able to connect your dots
life's problems can become a cancer,
I'm not exactly sure what your problem is
But, I know Jesus is your answer.
Don't let your problems get the best of you

it will tie your stomach in knots,
Give Jesus the swirling thoughts in your head
and trust Him to connect your dots.

Don't Be a Coward

You can't be a coward and follow Jesus,
He wants a warrior indeed
Put on the full armor of God,
He'll meet your every need.
I'm not saying the battle is easy
the struggle will take its toll,
Stand up for Jesus, He'll guard your heart
He'll bring peace to your soul.
You can't be a coward and a warrior too,
my friend, they just don't mix,
In the heat of the battle, trust in God,
there's no problem He can't fix.
The Bible gave us many examples
of people who were brave for the Lord,
You can't pick and choose, when to be brave
you must live and die by the sword.
The sword of the spirit, God's Holy Word
will help you be brave every day,
Take the time to seek divine guidance
and being a coward won't come into play.
You can't be a coward and follow Jesus
you'll burn in the fire for sure,
Only the brave who stay in the word
can keep their heart clean and pure.
It's not easy fighting off satan
and the fiery darts he throws your way,
But, be a brave soldier and trust in Jesus
and definitely take time to pray.
Don't be a coward, stand up for Jesus

Jesus wasn't a coward for you,
He bravely gave His life on the cross
so, its' the least a brave soldier should do.

Following Jesus

I wasn't where I should be
my life was out of sync,
While I wasn't a total disaster
I was certainly on the brink.
My footsteps were not headed
where God wanted them to go,
I had given my heart to Jesus
but I had refused to grow.
I wasn't being obedient
or sharing Jesus with the lost,
I was busy being selfish
and too worried about the cost.
I know God's instructions
are not hard to understand,
He simply said to follow Him
and be a Godly man.
Time and time again
I ventured on my own,
I missed many opportunities
for God's seeds to be sown.
Still, I had a deep desire
to be what God wanted me to be,
I remembered those two little words
when God said "follow me".
So, I asked God for forgiveness
and I opened up His word,
The more I read my Bible,
the more my heart was stirred.
I began to understand

the importance of God's plan,
How He wanted me to follow Him
and be a Godly man.
I put aside the useless things
I used to daily do,
I began to implement the things
my Bible taught me to.
I shared my love for Jesus
helping people who had needs,
It felt good to follow Jesus
and help Him plant His seeds.
Now I daily follow Jesus
I go wherever I am led,
Helping the homeless and the hurting,
making sure they are fed.
I lend a hand to the helpless
and share Jesus with the lost,
I follow Jesus wherever He leads
and I don't worry about the cost.

God in a Box

God, I'm letting you out of the box
you've been there way too long,
The only one I've hurt is me
still I know I've done you wrong.
I can't really hold you down
and it's not the right thing to do
For you're the God of the universe
even the box belongs to you.
I'm not sure why I try this tactic
even to me it seems a bit odd,
How could such a tiny little box
hold something as big as God.
We all know about Jack-in-the-box
But, God's a lot bigger than Jack,
Trying to limit such a big God
only gets my life out of whack.
I know better still I get lost
I allow satan to lead me astray,
I put God in His box and sit on top,
then live life my own way.
Still, I know He has all the answers
without Him I'd surely be lost,
Stuffing God inside of a box
can come at a mighty high cost.
I know it's wrong, I beg your forgiveness
for putting you in such a tiny place,
I know I'm only hurting myself
and making it hard to see your face.
Lord, I come to you today once more

my life's a mess and on the rocks,
I want your blessings on my life once again
so, I'm taking you back out of this box.

God's Garage

There is no fancy sports car
no dirt bikes or four wheel drives.
I don't see golf clubs or a kayak,
no guns or fancy knives.
There's not a wall of odds and ends
or a tool box by the door,
There's not a bag full of rags
or an oil spill on the floor.
There was nothing earthly to see
in this garage I was standing in,
Everything in God's garage
was to help me flee from sin.
There was a huge Bible in giant print
on a stand ten feet tall,
I saw pictures of Jesus on the cross
plastered all over the wall.
All God's children were welcome here
a welcome sign was on the door,
I felt the presence of the Lord
and it shook me to my core.
A band of angels were singing
and it sounded oh so sweet,
They sang songs of praise and worship
as they bowed down at God's feet.
I knew this was God's address
and not some strange mirage,
I wondered what must be inside
if this was just His garage.
There were no earthly things

A garage may usually store,
Once you get to heaven
you won't need them anymore.
You won't need a place for stuff
or a home for your souped up Dodge,
Only things that don't cause you to sin
are allowed in God's garage.
Come on in and join us, friend,
as soon as you've arrived,
We'll celebrate in God's garage
because your soul has been revived.
Then we'll open the inside door
that leads to God's heavenly home,
We'll walk the streets of gold together
and forever we will roam.

God's Grace

If life seems to be wearing you down
and you're tired from the frantic pace,
What you need is a gentle reminder
to relax in God's abundant grace.
Have your dreams become so illusive,
you're not sure it's still worth the chase?
Give it to God, let Him work it out
and relax in the goodness of His grace.
Is your job and family stressing you out
you're just looking for a safe happy place,
The answer, my friend, is to give it to Jesus
and bask in His goodness and grace.
Are you searching for the joy you once felt
but, you can't find even a trace,
There's room for you at the foot of the cross
to get filled with His glorious grace.
At the foot of the cross is where you surrender
and ask Jesus to forgive all your sins,
It's where you receive grace upon grace
and new life in Jesus begins.
Life can be hard and the path can get dark
there's plenty of trials to face,
Still, there's no doubt when you give it to God
He'll always extend you His grace.
There are times when your path gets rocky
the road seems impossible to trod,
Don't give up, His grace is sufficient
once you turn it all over to God.
No matter where you've been or what you've done

or how far you think you've gotten off base,
Give it to Jesus at the foot of the cross
and God will bless you with His unending grace.

God's Sea of Goodness

Swimming in the sea of God's goodness
I'm not just sure where to begin,
I feel so blessed to walk with God
His blessings never seem to end.
It doesn't really seem to matter
how far out to sea I go,
God's goodness always surrounds me
and His blessings continue to flow.
Still, sometimes I get a little weary
when I swim far away from shore,
I start basking in all God's goodness
and lose sight of what I'm swimming for.
I'm swimming in the sea of God's goodness
but I'm failing to soak it all in,
The more I fail to soak in God's goodness
the more often I fall prey to sin.
Still, God never seems to mind
rescuing me from my sin.
He throws a life jacket and forgives me
and starts flowing His blessings again.
I'm not sure if I'll ever understand
for to me it seems a bit odd,
How can I be fooled by the devil
while swimming in the goodness of God.
I'm just thankful for an endless sea
of goodness to swim in each day,
I'm just as thankful God rescues me
when I start drifting away.
I'm trying to swim away from sin

It's God's goodness I'm swimming toward,
I'm secure in the goodness of God
and the mercy and grace of the Lord.
I'll swim in the sea of God's goodness
and keep daily soaking it in,
God's goodness is an awesome place,
and it's how each day should begin.
I'm swimming in the sea of God's goodness
trying not to drift too far from shore,
But, I'm not worried if I start drowning,
God will throw me a life jacket once more.

God's so Good

The sun breaks through the morning sky
and the birds begin to sing,
I roll out of bed excited to see
what new blessings today will bring.
I've seen it time and time again
it's an endless trail for sure,
God showers me with His blessings
although my heart's not always pure.
It's a concept I can't fully grasp.
I'll never truly understand,
How can I fail God so often
and still live a life so grand.
I may not know a whole lot,
probably far less than I should,
But, I know I'm blessed each day I wake up
and I know my God is good.
He talks with me and comforts me
as we walk along life's way,
I often fail, but I'm getting better
at listening to what God has to say.
He forgives me for things I don't do
when I told Him that I would,
He never leaves or forsakes me
Yes, I serve a God who's good.
I hope you have Jesus in your heart
and I pray you have no doubt,
I want you to have the abundant blessings
of God's goodness I'm talking about.
God's Word says draw nigh to Him

and, He'll draw nigh to you,
I've put God to the test on this
I've found out His word holds true.
His goodness starts over with each sunrise
as He cracks open the morning sky,
Still, I'll never understand why He's so good to me
no matter how often or hard I try.

Jesus Juice

Life gets hard and you have no answer
It feels like there's no use,
No matter what your problem is
you need some Jesus juice.
Sometimes life beats you up,
sometimes you get beaten down,
Good news is you've got some help
if you've got Jesus juice around.
No one lives a perfect life
we all have a problem or two
The trouble starts when they gang up
and you have more than just a few.
Everybody has struggles to deal with
we each have problems of our own,
I'm telling you, friend, you need Jesus juice
so you don't face the world alone.
Some people face their problems alone,
while some have family and friends,
Either way get you some Jesus juice
to help sustain you till your trouble ends.
Maybe you're wondering what's this Jesus juice
because you can't find it at the store,
Well here's some help because it'll be easier
when you know what you're looking for.
You'll never find it at the local store
no matter how hard you look,
Jesus juice is only available
in the pages of God's holy book.
My friend, if you've got problems

and life is tightening the noose,
Grab your Bible and open it up
and drink you some Jesus juice.
All your problems won't disappear,
that's not the way God works,
But if you'll try this Jesus juice
you'll benefit from all its perks.
What you'll find is mercy and grace
and peace that the devil stole,
A little Jesus juice every day
is the answer to soothe your soul.
Now you know how to deal with problems
so, you really don't have an excuse,
Pick up that Bible and give it a chance
and drink you some Jesus juice.

Make Time for God

I feel blessed as I spring outta bed,
I realize it's a new day once more,
I take a shower and brew some coffee
grab a cup and I'm out the door.
I listen to tunes watching the sunrise
as I take my usual morning drive,
It's a beautiful day and I've got a job
It feels good just to be alive.
Once at work the whirlwind starts
I solve problems at a world record pace,
By day's end I'm asking myself
why I go through this crazy rat race.
I hurry home to find some peace
but, let me tell you a secret, my friend,
What I found when I arrived home
was a rat race all over again.
I realized today was the day
I promised I would cut the grass,
But, the neighbor borrowed my mower
now, it's completely out of gas.
Kid's soccer practice is in half an hour
and my wife isn't feeling well,
I think there was more peace at work
but, it's still too early to tell.
The bedroom toilet is running over
and the dog knocked over the trash.
Some kid is selling candy at my door
and I can't seem to find any cash.
My youngest daughter is in her playpen,

screaming and crying to be fed,
But there's a fire on the stove top
I need to tend to instead.
Not even another cup of coffee
can help to calm this storm,
I'm being honest when I tell you
this crazy scene is quite the norm.
It's hard to admit the truth sometimes
but, it's a real good place to start,
Sometimes, I'm afraid it's true
I don't put the horse before the cart.
I often get things out of whack
as I live my life each day,
I raise my head and jump outta bed
but I don't take the time to pray.
Life is loaded with challenges,
I'll surely need some Godly help.
Still, I try to do it all alone
instead of letting God guide each step.
Now my job will still be hectic
and problems at home won't go away,
But, I'm sure I can better handle life's stress
if I take time to stop and pray.
So, I'm going to make time for God
I'm making time to stop and pray,
It's the perfect way to start each morning
and help me have peace throughout my day.

Make Your House a Home

Home is where the heart is,
I'm sure most folks agree,
Yet it's nothing more than a house
if your heart's never been set free
You may have healthy children
and you may have a beautiful wife,
But unless you have Jesus in your heart,
you don't have abundant life.
The home should be a happy place
a safe haven so to speak,
You can make sure that happens
if it's Jesus you choose to seek.
Chaos is sure to happen
and difficulties will come your way,
But invite Jesus into your home
and He'll hear you when you pray.
Sometimes the storms of life will rage
as though they'll never cease,
Always look to God for help
and trust Him to give you peace.
The home is just a building
made of brick or wood,
Without the Lord inside your walls,
your house will be no good.
You can have kids and a beautiful wife
and a house full of expensive stuff,
Yet, if you house is without Jesus,
my friend, it won't ever be enough.
God created you and your family,

He gave you everything you own,
He never intended for you to solve
life's problems all alone.
Be the man God wants you to be
and make your house a home,
Let Jesus have control, my friend,
don't allow your heart to roam.
Your healthy children will appreciate it,
your beautiful wife will thank you, too,
For your home will always be a safe haven
when you let God be in charge of you.

On My Knees Again

Lord, I'm on my knees again
I know it's been a while,
Things I should have brought to you
I just threw them in a pile.
Now my pile has become so big
It'll take some time to pray,
I humbly come before you, Lord,
please hear these words I say.
I know you always hear my prayers
that's not exactly what I mean,
It's just that I fail you often
and my heart feels so unclean.
I've let the devil set up camp
in dark corners of my heart,
I've neglected to ask you for help
and, I've failed to do my part.
So, I'm on my knees again, Lord,
bringing you my guilt and shame,
Forgive me and cleanse me, Lord,
as I now call upon your name.
Wash me in your blood I pray
so I am clean once more,
I want to stay in your presence
to see the blessings you have in store.
Lord, I'm down on my knees again
asking you to take this pile
I neglected you and carried my problems
for far too many a mile.
I should have come a while ago

to ask you for this help,
Lord, forgive me for leaving out
this most important step.
Take these burdens and forgive me, Lord,
like you always seem to do,
Please rid me of my guilt and shame
so, I once again feel close to you.

Prayer Time

Lord, I know I can come to you
I know you always care,
It doesn't matter what I've done
you always hear my prayer.
When I've totally let you down
and done things I shouldn't do,
You open the flood gates to heaven
so my prayers can still get through.
I've had a need, Lord, many times
to come before your throne of grace,
Although I'm an unworthy sinner,
you still reveal your face.
I know the blood that Jesus shed
is why my prayers get through,
And when I ask for forgiveness
you'll clean my heart anew.
Lord, help me bring my prayers to you
as I deal with daily stress,
I am thankful when I leave you out
you love me nonetheless.
I'm so grateful you hear my prayers,
for I often let you down,
I pray when I need forgiveness
it's not the only time I come around.
I'm in awe Lord, you've been so good
the burdens I bear are few,
I want to pray with a joyful heart
when I give my thanks to you.
All my prayers go straight to you,

you hear each word I say,
Lord, help me to always come to you
to start and end each day.
Lord, you are loving, and you are kind
you're generous in all your ways,
It's you who gives me abundant life
so, I'll always give you praise.
I know I should always pray to you
yet, so often I seem to fail,
Help me to learn to lean on you
in the bad and good times as well.
I'm just thankful I can count on you
to always hear my prayer,
For you are God, and I'm your child,
that's how I know you truly care.

Simple Man, Simple Plan

I'm just a simple man
I try not to make life hard,
Along the way I faced some things
that left me battle scarred.
The only battles I seem to lose
are ones I face on my own,
The devil knows I'm easy prey
when I go into battle alone.
Although I hate to admit it,
God's armor gets left behind.
Then the battle I fight with satan
is a battle of a different kind.
Sure there's been a time or two
when I've won a battle by myself,
Still, they didn't bring God glory
or put a trophy on my shelf.
Going into battle alone
is like fishing without a rod
I just can't reel in the victories
unless I go into battle with God.
I've lost many battles fighting alone
I got some scars along my way,
God's my strength, so I put on my armor
and I try not to miss a day.
That's my simple plan as a simple man,
don't leave God's armor at home,
Your battles are much easier to fight
when you don't face them on your own.

The Main Dish

Jesus should be your main dish
so, don't push Him to the side,
In Him you'll find a good friend
in whom you can confide.
Don't treat Him like a stranger
and make Him some side dish,
He's not a genie in a bottle,
where you can make some wish
He's the meat and the potatoes
Jesus is the main dish, for sure,
You can't treat Him like a side dish
and hope to live a life that's pure.
Don't treat Jesus like your leftovers
He's much more than that, my friend,
He's the Alpha and Omega
who'll be with you till the end.
You can always count on Jesus
He's a friend who's tried and true,
There's no doubt He's the main dish
for He gave His life for you.
Don't brush these words aside
for you are guilty as am I,
We treat Jesus like a side dish
and we have no good reason why.
Jesus lived a perfect life
a life totally free from sin,
It's a mistake to push Him aside
and not make Him our best friend.
Still, for some strange reason

we try to do things on our own,
We treat Jesus as some side dish
like He never made His presence known.
We push aside His sacrifice
the greatest gift He could give,
We don't appreciate His awesome love
and the perfect life our Savior lived.
We don't seem to count our blessings,
we only recognize our loss,
We take for granted the blood He shed
when He died upon the cross.
I don't know about you, my friend,
but, I hold Jesus in high esteem,
There's no doubt He's the main dish,
I'm just a player on His team.
It's time we put Jesus first again
and not use Him to grant some wish,
For He's our Savior and the Risen Lord
and He should always be our main dish.

The Story of Jesus

The Son of God sent from heaven
born of a virgin birth,
He lived, died, then rose again,
to show us what our soul was worth.
He was the word and He was God
yet, He became a man,
He lived a perfect sinless life,
this was God's salvation plan.
Jesus gave His life for you and me
this was the Father's will,
He showed us how to live and love
before He died on Calvary's hill.
We know Christ died on the cross
to save us from our sin,
We also know He conquered death
when in three days, He rose again.
Yet, it's everything in between
from His birth to the empty grave,
That helps me to understand
what Jesus truly gave.
While always seeking the Father's will
He showed us how to live,
He showed us how to beat the devil
how to serve and how to give.
He healed the lame and the blind
and cleansed the leper along His way,
He calmed the seas and walked on water
and taught us how to pray.
The example Christ set with His perfect life

was a sacrifice for all mankind,
Everything He did was out in the open
so it wouldn't be hard to find.
God gave us a book to live by
we call it the Bible today,
He inspired prophets to write this book
and gave them the words to say.
It started with a virgin birth
and ended with an empty tomb,
It's a story of Jesus and His sacrifices
to save the world from certain doom.
I tell you this story for you may not know
Jesus came to save mankind,
You may not know He inspired the prophets
so His truths would be easy to find.
My friend, if you don't know Jesus,
please open a Bible today,
Let His truths sink into your heart
because Jesus is the only way.
Along the way, Jesus made sacrifices
as He lived life here on earth,
He went through a lot of trouble, my friend,
to prove what our soul's really worth.

Section Eight

MATTERS OF THE HEART

For Reflection:

It's most important to give your heart to Jesus, still we all have that special someone that moves our heart. It is a true gift from God.

And the Lord God said, It is not good that the man should be alone; I will make him an help meet for him.

—Genesis 2:18

Matters of the Heart

All In or All Out

Maybe I'm not qualified
to have my thoughts heard,
Some of my ideas on the subject
Even to me, seem a bit absurd.
When it comes to having relationships
I'm usually all out or all in,
That's why I find it particularly hard
to have a woman as my friend.
I've got a few so it can be done
it's the dynamics that come into play,
Especially when you're attracted to her
and she don't feel the same way.
Some guys like to stick around
hoping one day she'll change her mind,
Not me, I choose to move along
and see what else I can find.
Some people say that's a cowardly way,
and I'll certainly respect their view,
It's best if I do what's good for me
and you do what's best for you.
It's back to all in, all out for me
I'm a committed kind of guy,
Give your all and if it don't' work
there's still time to say goodbye.
I know it's a totally different game
that brings many trials and tests,
But the heart never really comes alive
until it learns how to invest.
You can have fun enjoying each other

and even have a friendship too,
For me it's kinda like riding the fence
and I never quite know what to do.
That's why I just hang with the guys
it's a much less complicated deal,
There's no hormones, and a lot less drama
and I'm not worried about sex appeal.
Problem is there's a lot of good women
ones that aren't within my grip,
Even though it may not turn into love
I may miss out on a great friendship.
So, I'm all in and I'll go all out
though it's a different way to invest,
I'm no fence rider, but I'll give it a try
and let God take care of the rest.

Door to the Heart

The heart can only be filled by God
for it's He who made our heart,
But, He made a room with a special door
so people could play a big part.
The door to the heart will open wide
when a special love exists,
A special someone that when they're gone
it seems they're always missed.
Your feelings will prompt the door,
and it will swing open wide,
You'll allow that special someone
to share what you have inside.
Not just anyone is allowed inside
to roam around for free,
No, they must truly be special
and have a special key.
Every heart has a combination
that opens that special door,
The combination will be your key
if you have what they're looking for.
There's a special need in every heart
and every heart is made unique,
Yet, every heart has a common goal
to reach love's highest peak.
It's true only God can fill the heart
for He designed the heart that way,
Still, He made a room with a special door,
that's where you and I come into play.
Don't give up on love, my friend

I know you've been hurt before,
People broke in and damaged your lock
using the wrong key to your door.
One day God will send a special someone
they'll possess that special key,
They'll have the combination to your heart, and
things will be as they should be.
God always has a purpose and a plan
it's the same with matters of the heart,
He created the door to that special room
but we still have to do our part.
Trust in God and trust His plan
keep your heart clean and pure,
Look out your window, at your special door,
God will send someone special for sure.

Just Maybe

I saw the beauty in her eyes
it blew my heart away,
What must I do to win her over
so she'll always want to stay.
I know I haven't known her long
yet, it feels like all my life.
The beauty I see deep in her heart
are the traits of a Godly wife.
I wonder why God sent her my way
and if she is meant for me,
Only time will tell God's plan
so, we both must wait and see.
So far so good, I must admit
I'm overwhelmed for sure,
I'm taken in by her magic spell
and there may not be a cure.
I don't really want a cure
in fact, I'm quite content.
I just want to protect the heart
of this angel God has sent.
I'll take her beauty, I'll take my time
and let this angel fly along,
I'll try to show her the man I am
and that I'll never do her wrong.
Who knows, if I play my cards right
in this crazy game of life,
Maybe I'll mend her broken wing
and one day she'll be my wife.

Love Never Fails

Love is patient, love is kind,
yes it's a many splendored thing,
Still, there's one thing we all expect
love never seems to bring.
God's Word tells us love never fails
so we push love to the brink,
We seem to think love just happens
we don't take time to stop and think.
Love does not envy, or seek its own
it doesn't puff up or ever boast,
To love like God says we should
it's God we must love the most.
Bear all things, believe all things
hope and endure things till the end,
Unless we're seeking God for help
we can't accomplish this, my friend.
I may move mountains with my faith
whether I move them in whole or part,
I still have nothing without love
and its effects to rule my heart.
I may take my worldly possessions
to go and feed the poor,
I may rejoice in truth and suffer long
those are good things to do I'm sure.
Yet, we can never obtain that one thing
although we often tend to boast,
What we want is love that never fails
that's the one thing we want the most.
Yes, we brag, but we will never know

true love without knowing God,
We can never know how to truly love
unless it's God's path we trod.
God is love and He's all the things
that love could ever be,
He sacrificed His Son on Calvary's cross
so the world could plainly see.
There's only one love that never fails
it's God's love for you and me,
The unending love of the risen Lord
and He offers it to us for free.

The Heart's Dilemma

You win some, you lose some
and some just slip away,
There's no telling what may happen
when the heart strings are in play.
It is more than meets the eye
in almost every case,
When you're dealing with your feelings,
it can be a scary place.
Sharing your heart with another
can make you feel quite prone,
So you keep your thoughts inside
and the truth is never known.
You self-preserve and self-protect
you've felt that pain before.
You make sure to protect your heart
no matter who comes to your door.
But, then again, the heart's not made
to keep it to yourself,
It only serves one purpose
if you put it on a shelf.
To experience the fruits of life
you must open up your heart,
It's a difficult task, my friend,
yet, that's how love gets its start.
Sure you can preserve and self-protect
and build yourself a wall,
You may not think it's worth the risk
it's up to you to make that call.
Just ask yourself this one question

before you decide which way you'll go,
Has your heart experienced all there is,
or is there still room for it to grow.

The Real Deal

Your love for me feels oh so sweet,
But, the love from God can't be beat.
I can't explain how you make me feel,
I only know your love feels real.
You don't have to change, just be you,
I feel special from the things you do.
Even still, it is God I seek,
It's God's love that knows no peak.
Your love's awesome, but the truth be told,
Only the love of God soothes my soul.
Your love for me is awesome, I know,
But places in my heart only God can go.
Love's climb with you is a climb to keep,
Yet it's God's love that's wide and deep.
I desire your love, yet better still
It's God's love that seals the deal.
Your love for me is sweet for sure,
It feels authentic and it feels pure.
But, what I truly seek comes from above,
Yes, it is God for God is love.
God made me and gave me a soul,
He made my heart and created a hole.
No matter how special your love may be,
Only God can fill that hole in me.

The Right One

How many times must I fall in love
to finally find the right one,
It seems I'm captured in the web
of the magic spell that's spun.
At first it always seems so right,
but, then it falls apart,
I get entangled in her magic web
and soon she breaks my heart.
Try as I may to get away
from the entrapment she has set,
It don't take long to realize
there's nothing left here but regret.
What must I do to escape this web
and finally find true love,
The key for sure is to trust in God
and get help from up above.
Still, I try to solve my problem
and do it on my own,
I wind up captured in her web
broken hearted and all alone.
I think I'll find the right one
every time I get away,
I probably would if I'd turn to God
and take time to stop and pray.
I'm not sure why I ignore God
and put my trust in me,
I've only made a mess of love,
that's plain for everyone to see.
Still, I keep diving in head first

getting entangled once again,
Refusing to ask God for help
or letting Jesus be my friend.
I could keep getting captured
in the web that she has spun,
My heart would continue to break
and I wouldn't ever find the right one.
But, now I've found the answer
and discovered Jesus is the key,
So, it's time to put my trust in Him
and let Him find the right one for me.

Uncomplicated Mess

Can you properly define love
so that everyone would agree,
For what loves means to someone else
may not mean the same to me.
It's not that complicated friend
unless you decide to make it that way,
All you must do is reach in your heart
and put the love you have in play.
I'm not sure if I'd win a debate
should you challenge my point of view,
Love seldom seems to sail smooth waters
there's usually a problem or two.
At the very least we'd all agree
love can certainly cause you stress,
It's beautiful, yet still perplexing,
it's just an uncomplicated mess.
Love truly is uncomplicated
until your heart gets hung out to dry
Then you make a mess trying to figure out
how to give love another try.
Still, I think love is uncomplicated
at the same time it's just a mess,
How it can be one and still be the other
I suppose that's anyone's guess.
I'll tell you about my messy love
as uncomplicated as it may be,
The only reason I can deal with the mess
Is because I always have Jesus with me.
No matter how messy love is for you,

Jesus is the answer for sure,
Just let Jesus give you a hand
and love will be easier to endure.
Don't get bogged down in messy love
and let it cause you too much stress
Give it to Jesus, He'll show you the way
to uncomplicate your complicated mess.

Section Nine

SPREADING THE WORD

For Reflection:

If you really love Jesus, somewhere along your way, you can't help but share with others what He's done for you.

But sanctify the Lord God in your hearts: and be ready always to give an answer to every man that asketh you a reason of the hope that is in you with meekness and fear.

—I Peter 3:15

Spreading the Word

A Soldier for God

I am a soldier in God's army
there's nothing I can't endure,
I strive to please the Lord
and live a life that's clean and pure.
Each day I clean my gun
and polish up my boots,
To be a good soldier in God's army,
He must be able to see my fruits.
Every morning when I wake up
I make sure my barracks are clean,
I keep everything nice and tidy
so Jesus can be easily seen.
My uniform gets a little dirty
and my boots get muddy, too.
Sometimes I'm out of line
in the things I choose to do.
I allow a little dirt and grime
to creep into my gun,
I might even stumble a bit
as I make my daily run.
I'm not a perfect soldier,
no matter how hard I try,
But I'll be a soldier in God's army
until the day I die.
I'm ready to go to battle
every morning I lift my head,
I won't quit when I get dirty,
I'll get forgiveness from God instead.
God knows being in His army

is an obstacle course for sure,
He knows I may stumble a bit
to live a life that's clean and pure.
That won't stop me from being God's soldier
and it won't keep God from loving me,
So, each day I'll clean my barracks
and go be the best soldier I can be.

A Willing Heart

Lord, help me now your will to do
I want to walk close to thee,
I'll go wherever the Spirit leads
so, please clearly reveal to me.
My heart is willing to follow you
I know you know what's best,
I pray you brightly light my path
and help me pass your test.
I know you'll guide me if I'll trust
still it's not an easy task,
You never fail, you're always there
no matter how often I ask.
It's not the first time I've needed help
I've let you down before I know,
Yet, you showed mercy and gave me grace
And each day you help me grow.
The path gets narrow, and I get weak,
that's why I come today,
I am no good Lord when I'm alone
I need you to guide my way.
Here I stand Lord yet once again
not knowing just what to do,
Show me your will and light my path
Lord help me trust and follow you.
I thank you Lord well in advance
I know you'll soon reveal,
It's your purpose that I follow you
and walk within your will.
So, keep me humble and give me peace

until I can clearly see,
I know you'll brightly light my path
and show your will to me.
I guess that's all Lord, you know the rest
you always do your part,
You'll light my path and reveal your will
you only need my willing heart.
So my heart is yours yet once again
as I pray this prayer today,
I am thankful through all my failures
you still lead and guide my way.

Arise

Arise from your sleep, my friend,
and step into God's light,
He's calling you to serve
and His timing is always right.
You have been spiritually dead
since you gave your heart to Christ,
Still, the Holy Spirit is calling
don't make Him call you twice.
Although you haven't shared your faith
or hardly made a peep,
The Lord can still use you
if you'll awaken from your sleep.
Jesus wants to use you
but you must listen to His call.
You're still a child of the King
and He loves us one and all.
God gave you many talents
He has a purpose just for you,
He'll bless your life and others
if you do what He asks you to.
Don't think God can't use you
because you've been asleep to long.
That's not what God's Word says
and His word is never wrong.
God's Word says you're His handiwork
His word is tried and true,
So, awaken from your spiritual sleep
and let God start using you

Daily Chore

From one horizon to the other
from the morning to the evening shore,
I rise each day to follow Jesus
I've made this my daily chore.
Don't let the word I use bother you
It's a chore I love to do,
My friend, I hope following Jesus
is a chore that you enjoy too.
As the sun rises to start my day
until it disappears each night,
I pray I follow in the footsteps of Jesus
and serve Him with all my might.
I do have other daily chores
that bring structure to my life as well,
But, my priority is to follow Jesus
and help save lost souls from hell.
I'd like to say I've mastered this chore
but friend, that's simply not the case,
There's plenty of days I serve myself
and I don't seek the Father's face.
Still, following Jesus is my daily goal
and He forgives my human flaw,
His love and forgiveness humble me
I truly am in awe.
So, onward I go aiming for the prize
and Jesus is in the lead,
The more diligent I am doing my job
the more Jesus fills my need.
Each day I rise to follow Jesus

it's my most important daily chore,
I pray I follow in His footsteps
and walk through every open door.
I'm thankful Jesus always loves me
He's there to help with my daily chore,
I can't wait for a new horizon
to see what blessings He has in store.

Fishing for Men

You probably think of lures and bait
when it's fishing your thinking about,
You dream of catching a big ole bass or
filling your cooler with trout.
Now catching fish can be a lot of fun,
setting the hook and reeling 'em in,
Jesus showed me a different way to fish
Now I go fishing for men.
Don't get me wrong, I still like to fish
and set the hook on a big ole bass,
I love the challenge and being in nature
it's a great way to make time pass.
I still go fishing from time to time
but it feels like a while since I've been,
Now whenever I have free time
I go fishing for men.
I'll never sell my boat, I'll always fish,
It's a manly kind of thing to do,
There's something about being on the water
and the calm of an early morning view.
That being said there is much more meaning
when I go fishing for men,
The fields are plentiful, the fishermen are few
and the world is drowning in sin.
There's a special feeling fishing with God
I don't even set the hook,
All I do is go where He leads
and share the truths in His book.
The Holy Spirit keeps touching hearts

and winning the souls of men,
I just share the meat of His word
and Jesus keeps reeling em in.
Maybe you'd like to go fishing with me
there's plenty of room in my boat
The blessings you'll get is a spiritual high
that will keep your heart afloat.
Even if you don't it won't slow me down
I'll still consider you my friend,
Maybe I'll see you out fishing for bass
after I get through fishing for men.

Follow Me

The world is filled with temptation
and enticing things to see,
Yet, I keep hearing God speak the words
my son, come follow me.
Choosing to live a sinful life
is not a choice I can afford,
What must I do to ward off satan
and listen to the Lord.
God wants me to follow Him
so He can lighten my load
satan wants to tempt me with sin
that leads down a dead end road.
I know the answer is to lean on God
and put my trust in Him,
but I can't follow in His footsteps
if it's done on just a whim.
To follow Jesus it takes dedication
and a heart full of desire,
If I'll ask Jesus for a helping hand
He'll set my soul on fire.
It's not just me that Jesus wants
He wants you to follow as well,
He wants to give you an abundant life
and save your soul from hell.
He'll bless your life in many ways
like you've never seen before,
So, start each day with Jesus
and see the blessings He has in store.
It's not easy to be a Christian

and crawl out on that limb.
My friend, it totally changed my life
when I chose to follow Him.
I still have to fight off satan
you'll have to fight him too,
Don't worry if you're following Jesus
He'll fight those battles for you.
Come to Jesus today, my friend,
let Him lighten your load
Stop letting satan rule your life
and lead you down a dead end road.
It's an easy formula, yet a narrow path
God gave to set us free,
Still, I pray you make Jesus your Savior
the next time He says come follow me.

Fruits of the Spirit

What if you saw your life as a reflection
of all the things you chose to be,
What kind of a picture do you think
you will leave for others to see?
Do you live in such a way
that God's love can truly grow?
Do you share His love with others
no matter where you may go?
Does the joy that comes from God
follow your life around?
Do you find when you speak
you always make a joyful sound?
Do you have the peace of God
so to others you can give?
Do you share God's awesome peace
in the way you daily live?
Are you able to suffer long
to help your fellow man?
Do you reach out to others
and do the best job you can?
Do you show your gentle side
when life's beating down on you?
Do you show goodness to your neighbor
in the little things you do?
Do you have a faith in God
that moves mountains from your path?
Are you able to maintain that faith
even when you feel God's wrath?
Do you possess the many qualities

that a meek person might display?
Are you humble and submissive
and obedient along your way?
Do you exhibit temperance in your life
with self-restraint and self-control?
Can you claim these fruits of the Spirit
is that even part of your goal?
I know it's important to each of us
what others in our life see,
Still, its most important we understand
this is how God says we should be.
God gave us these nine little goals
of how we should treat our fellow man,
It's a good idea to choose one each day
and try to perform it the best you can.
If you'll follow this plan for a little while
and don't expect your results too quick,
God will surely bless you, my friend,
and you'll soon have some fruit to pick.

Living for Jesus

I'm getting older but that's okay
I'm not finished yet, my friend,
I still plan to enjoy life
up until the very end.
I may only have a year or two
but hopefully many more.
I'm not God, so I don't know
exactly what's in store.
I've certainly lived a good life
I've been blessed along the way,
The best way I can honor God
is to live for Him today.
What I do each day is important
I shouldn't live on just a whim,
I'll thank God each day I rise
and go live my life for Him.
That looks different for each of us
for God has a flexible plan,
It's important to find your purpose
then go make your daily stand.
It may be at work or the grocery store
or the many places in between,
Always remember to live today
so the love of Jesus is seen.
One thing for sure, you're sending a message
and you want it to be loud and clear,
Take the time to share Jesus with others
and show them your love's sincere.
Sure, I'm getting older, and so are you

300

with every day God lifts our head,
Today's important, don't live on a whim,
go live it for Jesus instead.

Lord Help Me

Lord, you've always been there,
you've helped me so many times,
You fill my mind, you fill my heart
and you inspire me with these rhymes.
Lord, help me as I rise each morning
your will I'll continue to see.
Guide my path and my purpose
and, illuminate your will for me.
Lord, help me to trust that you
will make things crystal clear,
So, I can share Jesus with others
when I feel frozen by my fear.
Lord, help me to be humble
and admit when I am wrong,
Gently remind me I'm your child
and that I always will belong.
Lord, I'm grateful and thankful
for the times you've been there,
There's no way to ever keep count
of all the times you've shown you care.
I thank you for my talent,
I thank you for your awesome love,
I thank you for the assurance,
I have a home in heaven above.
I thank you for your sacrifice,
that came at such a high cost,
For without the blood of Jesus Christ
the whole world would be lost.
I know there's much more, Lord

for your goodness never ends,
I thank you for your mercy and grace
and forgiveness from all my sins.
Lord, I'm thankful for all this
but, I still need your daily help,
I need you to walk beside me
and to guide my every step.
Lord, help me to use my talents
and glorify your Holy name,
I know when people turn to you,
they'll never again be the same.
Lord, help me to share your blessings
through these poems and rhymes,
Lord, help me to share in such a way
so, they'll change many hearts and minds.

The Answer

When the storms of life roll in
and your world gets tossed about,
Nothing seems to go your way
you're consumed by fear and doubt.
You're not sure if life's worth living,
there's no blue sky in sight,
You feel you've taken your best shot
and you're weary from the fight.
Friend, I know exactly how you feel,
I've been down that road before,
Hardship and hurt have no boundaries,
it visits the rich as well as the poor.
The Bible paints a beautiful picture
of a Savior born long ago,
I want to introduce you to Him
in case somehow you don't know.
Jesus is always the answer, my friend,
no matter what your problem may be,
He died upon a cross for all
He died for both you and me.
He knew life would toss us around
and we'd struggle to conquer sin,
So, He shed His blood and died for us
and in three days He rose again.
It's the love story of the Bible
Jesus displayed till His last breath,
Now our sins can be forgiven
because Jesus conquered death.
When your life gets tossed around

when storms clouds come rolling in,
Remember, you have a Savior who died
to save you from your sin.
Jesus will help you fight your battle
and find blue skies like before,
He'll take away the weight of sin
and help you feel alive once more.
That's the power of the cross,
it's a debt you can't repay,
But, it's a gift, you can't buy it
because Jesus don't work that way.
He offers us eternal life
so our problems don't bog us down,
He comes to live inside our heart
He knows that's how true peace is found.
Give your heart to Jesus, my friend
replace storms with blue skies again,
Everyone knows life is so much better
when you get forgiveness from your sin.

The Great Commission

I'm well aware there's a good chance
I'm about to step on some toes,
But, it's an important question
so that's just the way it goes.
Is the love you have for Jesus
buried deep in your heart,
Or are you sharing it with others
and doing your appointed part?
Now, I'm not trying to judge you,
but it's important for you to know,
That you're sharing the love of Jesus
with people wherever you go.
I'm talking about the Great Commission,
that's exactly the subject at hand,
God clearly laid it out for us
so we could easily understand.
I know it's important to live it out
and let others see Jesus in you,
Still, God's Word clearly points out
that's not the only thing we should do.
It can be hard to share your faith
in this world so filled with sin,
Maybe you don't feel well equipped
and you're not sure just where to begin.
I've felt that way, and sometimes I still do
trying to share Jesus face to face,
God always provides the right words to say
when I get in that scary place.
He'll do the same for you, my friend,

for we're commissioned to go and teach,
Anything God tells us to do for Him
always has an answer within our reach.
It can be daunting to share your faith
venturing into something that's new,
The harvest in this sinful world is plentiful
and the workers who share are few.
You may think you're doing your part
by living life in a Godly way,
Still, the Great Commission makes it clear
with the words Jesus had to say.
We're to go, and we're to teach
and baptize in the name of Jesus,
If you get filled with the Holy Spirit
you'll want others to know how it frees us.
So, live a good life and live for God
and let others see Jesus in you,
But, the Great Commission says go and teach,
and that's exactly what you should do.

Section Ten

HOME SWEET HOME

For Reflection:

> We may not know exactly what heaven will look like, but we know we'll be with Jesus, and *it don't get any better than that.*

> And if I go and prepare a place for you, I will come again, and receive you unto myself; that where I am, there ye may be also.
>
> —John 14:3

Home Sweet Home

Come Home

There's many a reason as I've walked this earth,
I've allowed my heart to roam,
Yet, no matter how far I got from God,
I always found my way back home.
It didn't matter how often I strayed,
or how far off the path I trod,
I always knew if I'd just come home,
I could still be used by God.
Home is where the heart is,
and my heart is at heaven's door,
I'm trying to focus on my purpose
so I don't stray away anymore.
That's probably not very realistic,
for the human heart tends to roam.
I'm just grateful Jesus never forsakes me,
and He always welcomes me home.
Not only am I always welcomed home,
but the door is open wide.
All I must do is show up,
and take a step back inside.
God will have a fireplace going,
He'll have some burgers on the grill
It's always celebration time
when we show up to do God's will.
So, if you've strayed away from heaven's door
and you're feeling lost and all alone,
My friend, don't delay, return today;
God will always welcome you home.

Heavenly Horsepower

I won't be the least bit worried
when I face my final hour,
Jesus gave me a full supply
of His good heavenly horsepower.
It's true I may not need it
once I walk through heaven's door,
But, there's no way I'm living without it
until I reach that final shore.
Look a little closer and you'll see
it's what keeps my life intact,
It's how I deal with problems
and, my friend, that's just a fact.
If this heavenly horse power's so great,
I guess you wonder how it works,
You want to figure how to get some
and how to tap into its perks.
Well, I can tell you all about it
how its wonders never cease,
How getting good heavenly horsepower
helps you find your earthly peace.
How heavenly horsepower gives you traction
no matter the storm you're in,
How it'll be your saving grace
when you're struggling in your sin.
How it'll bring you joy and love
like you never knew before,
How there'll be nothing to compare it to
until you walk through heaven's door.
See, long ago God made a promise

He'd never send another flood,
Then He sent His only Son Jesus
to sacrifice His precious blood.
Now we can have heavenly horsepower
if we'll call upon His name,
He'll fill us with heavenly horsepower
and life won't ever be the same.
You can use it while here on earth
but, it's a gift for eternal life,
It's God's way to help His children
deal with their earthly strife.
There's an endless supply, don't even ask why
just get you some today,
Your heavenly horsepower awaits in Jesus
He's the truth, the life, the way.
I share this truth for one simple reason
so you don't live life bitter and sour,
I want you to be free, saved like me
enjoying God's gift of heavenly horsepower.

My Heavenly 401k

I used to gather earthly treasures
but, now I don't tuck them away,
I gather treasures with eternal value
for my heavenly 401k.
I thought material things were important,
now I've finally figured it out,
Sharing Jesus and saving souls
is how I earn my heavenly clout.
Things and stuff are a part of life
but we must be careful, my friend,
When we make those things our God,
is when our heart falls prey to sin.
Everyone desires an abundant life
we want to enjoy the fruits of our labor,
Still, we're storing up the wrong treasures
if we don't share Jesus with our neighbor.
Jesus said I'll be known by my fruits
they're always there for Him to see,
If I seek the kingdom of heaven first
all these things will be added to me.
I want to store up treasures in heaven
so one day I'll hear Jesus say,
Well done my good and faithful servant
you've built quite a heavenly 401k.
I'll go to church and sow good seeds
I'll be kind to the people I meet,
I'll give my time and use my talents
to be Jesus's hands and feet.
I'll help the homeless and the hurting

and lend the widow a hand,
I'll hand out Bibles and smiles too
I'll help the lost to understand.
I'll still enjoy life here on earth
but remember sharing Jesus is the way,
To store up treasures in Heaven
and build up my heavenly 401k.
Make no mistake, I'll be far from perfect
I certainly won't do everything right,
Still, my goal will be sharing Jesus
and trying to be salt and light.
I know my works won't save me
the main thing that will come into play,
Is surrendering to Jesus and living for Him
that's the cornerstone of my 401k.
That's why I gave Jesus my heart
He's my Savior, I have no doubt,
Now I'm sharing Jesus and saving souls
and building up my heavenly clout.
I no longer stress over earthly treasures
I now know Jesus is truly the way,
So, I spend my days doing all I can
to build up my heavenly 401k.

My Heavenly Angel

An angel lives on my windowsill,
it stays there day and night
I know because he always checks
to make sure that I'm alright.
I'm certain it is an angel
from the heavenly way it glows,
No matter how far I roam each day
my angel always goes.
When I return and crawl into bed
my angel's back in sight,
Sitting on my windowsill
giving off his glorious light.
He's more than just a heavenly angel
sitting on my windowsill,
he's my protector and my guide
as I seek to do God's will.
Lord, I've neglected many times
to thank you for this special gift,
Still, I'm grateful for my angel,
and how he makes my spirits lift.
I could never fully explain to you
how my blessings never end,
There's no doubt I'm not worthy
to have an angel as my friend.
I know I'm not alone
you probably have an angel too,
God put one on your windowsill
so he could keep an eye on you.
Lord, thank you for your angels

I certainly need their help
On my windowsill and as I roam
to guide my every step.
I truly am grateful, Lord
for my angel's heavenly glow,
I know I'd be totally lost
if my angel should ever go.
Of all the many places
this angel could have flown,
he landed on my windowsill
to make his presence known.
So good night my heavenly angel
I'll rest well here in your sight,
Knowing God put you on my windowsill
to keep me safe throughout the night.

No More

There'll be no more weeping and disappointment,
no more sorrow and pain,
No more daily little problems
to always tax your brain.
There'll be no more sweeping and mopping,
no more laundry to fold,
No more doctor's appointment to keep,
I won't worry about growing old.
There'll be no more raking and mowing the yard,
worrying about that spot I missed,
It's going to be awesome in heaven
with no more honey-do list.
There'll be no more worrying about kids
no more decisions to make,
No more trying to keep yourself healthy
no more medication to take.
There'll be no more traffic and no road rage,
no more stressing to get to work,
No more dealing with favoritism
and your boss acting like a jerk.
There'll be no more hurting and homeless people
no more singing the blues,
No more dealing with hopeless addiction
no more drugs and no more booze.
There'll be no more problems to figure out
no more wondering how and why,
No more worries and no more needs
no more just barely getting by.
There'll be no more stress when we get to heaven

it just won't exist anymore,
There'll be no more worldly drama
only blessings will be in store.
So hang on, those no-more days are coming
I don't think it's going to be long,
There'll be no more time to change your mind
if you got this whole thing wrong.
Trust me you don't want to be wrong
and miss out on the beauty of no more,
Accept Jesus today so you'll know
exactly what you're living for.
Please don't miss your ticket to heaven
so you can walk thru heaven's door,
Once that trumpet sounds and the final curtain falls,
There'll be no more time to prepare for no more.

On my way to Heaven

I know where I am headed
Lord, help me not to roam,
Keep me on the straight and narrow
for heaven is my home.
I can't wait to join the angel choir
and praise your holy name,
I know once I get to heaven
things won't ever be the same.
I'm on my way to heaven
I certainly know the way,
I'm on my way to heaven
I get closer every day.
I'm on my way to heaven
where my riches are untold,
I'm on my way to heaven
to walk the streets of gold.
I know I'll see my loved ones
and we'll rejoice in one accord,
We'll spend eternity together
in the joy of the Lord.
I won't ever have far to go
to come before God's throne,
That's the way He designed it
when heaven is your home.
I'm on my way to heaven
Lord, you're the captain of my ship,
I'm on my way to heaven
I can't wait to take that trip.
I'm on my way to heaven

My ship is yours to steer,
I'm on my way to heaven
where my troubles will disappear.
Every day I think of heaven
where mansions in glory await,
I'll have no more pain and suffering,
no more sin and no more hate.
I'll be signed, sealed, and delivered
to my heavenly home above,
I'm on my way to heaven
there is nothing there but love.
When I hear that trumpet sound
I won't have to wonder why,
It will be a glorious day
when I meet Jesus in the sky.
I'll be on my way to heaven
for heaven is my home
It's time to stand accountable
And see the seeds I've sown.
I'll finally be up in heaven,
walking those streets of gold,
Singing praises to my Jesus,
and it never will grow old.
My soul will be at perfect peace
for Christ claimed me as His own,
I'm no longer on my way to heaven
I have finally made it home.

The Hope of Heaven

This won't be the last time I see you
as we lay you in this grave,
You opened up your heart to Jesus,
and your soul was there to save.
You lived a changed life for sure
once you let Jesus have control,
I know your soul's rejoicing in heaven
as we bury you in this hole.
That don't stop my heart from hurting
for your body's no longer here,
Now all I have left to love
are the memories I hold so dear.
I'm at peace when I think of you,
I know you're where you belong,
I'll go on with just your memory,
and ask the Lord to keep me strong.
I don't know how or when,
maybe morning, noon, or night,
It may be days, or maybe years
but no doubt we'll reunite.
I gave my heart to Jesus, too,
He saved my soul from hell,
I know we'll meet again someday
but for now only time will tell.
Enjoy your awesome heavenly home
rest well my dear sweet friend,
I'll hold onto our memories
knowing this is not our end.
One day God will claim my soul,

and they'll bury me next to you,
That's the hope of heaven I have
once my life on earth is through.

The Narrow Path

The Bible tells me Jesus keeps
His eye on every little sparrow,
That makes it easy for me to believe
He'll help me walk the straight and narrow.
This is the path that God requires
to enter into heaven's gate,
It's no easy task, my friend,
if your priorities are not straight.
Many a soul has passed away
yet did not make it in,
They detoured on the broad path
and got consumed by all their sin.
Make no mistake, it's no easy journey
and only a few make this trek,
You can't make it on your own
for ole satan has stacked the deck.
We all stumble from time to time
some more, some a little less,
The problem comes from the selfish soul
who tries to clean up their own mess.
If we're to walk the narrow path
Jesus is the help we'll need,
We'll have to walk in His footsteps
and allow Him to take the lead.
It just won't work any other way
no matter how hard you try,
satan will steer you off your path,
my friend, he's way too sly.
If you walk the straight and narrow

the rewards are oh so sweet,
You get to enter heaven's gate
and sit at the Master's feet.
A mistake we seem to often make
as we try and walk this path,
Is thinking we have to be perfect
or we're going to feel God's wrath.
Sometimes we feel God's mighty wrath
for the many times we fail,
But, we feel His mercy and His grace
and His awesome love as well.
God never expected our perfection
as we walk life's narrow path,
So, He sent His Son to shed His blood
and cleanse us with a spiritual bath.
The times we act less than perfect
we come to God and confess,
We pray for Him to forgive us
and He always cleans up our mess.
Never forget the blood of Jesus
is always there for us to use,
Still, do your best, when you confess,
it's not meant to be abused.
It matters not if you're rich or poor
if you have a big house or an fancy car,
God wants you to walk the narrow path
so, come and follow Him just as you are.
His eye is on every little sparrow
He sees you too, my friend,

Do your best to follow the narrow path
and never give up till the end.
When you feel weak, turn to God
and ask Him to give you some help.
He'll be there to lead your way
and He'll guide your every step.

About the Author

 Travis Jenkins is the middle son in a family of three boys. He was born and raised in the South and is the proud father of one son, Todd Austin Jenkins. Travis is a former high school all-American baseball player. He played ball at the University of Mississippi and Union University, where he majored in journalism and was a sportswriter for the local paper while he attended college. He was a long-time member at Oakhurst Baptist Church, where he served as a church member, and was part of the softball team, a nine-time state championship-winning team, from 1990-1999.

Travis was selected by the American Softball Association (ASA) as an All-American player in 1999, recognizing him as one of the nation's outstanding softball players. It was his love for sports and competition that kept a ball in his hand and a pen out of it for many years. Travis spent thirty years in the railroad industry and is currently enjoying his retirement from this career. His free time is spent volunteering at the local mission and helping the homeless, hungry, and hurting people of his community in Mobile, Alabama. When he's not helping the needy and sharing Jesus, he enjoys golf, the great outdoors, and spending time with friends and family. He creates poetry almost daily and most recently, is inspired to write songs and create music that honors God.

More from the Author

Christian Rhymes for Trying Times, Book One. Available on Amazon.

Songs of Truth, Original Soundtrack by Singer/Songwriter Travis Jenkins. Search: Youtube.com/Music by Travis Jenkins. Provided by CDBaby. Original CD Also available (while supplies last) by contacting the author.

Invite Travis to speak at your Church, Men's Group, or Bible Study. Contact Travis Jenkins via email at: JesusJourney22@ gmail.com.

Personal Testimony

I feel very fortunate and blessed. I was raised in a Christian home by parents who loved the Lord. They made sure I knew who Jesus was and what He did for me on the cross. At the age of 11, I felt the Holy Spirit speak to my heart. The decision to give my heart to Jesus and get baptized secured my place in Heaven for eternity (Ref: John 3:16).

Until I was 16, my dad was in the ministry, and our family moved *a lot*. Every year or so, we were moving to a new town and a new everything. Learning how to adapt, adjust, and fit in was a challenge for me as a teenager. I can't say how much this contributed to my straying from the straight and narrow, but I know I wanted to be liked and accepted by the new people I met, so I was a little mischievous. I never strayed too far, but I certainly allowed worldly things to become more important than my relationship with God (Ref: Matthew 6: 19-21).

I have many stories I could share about being on fire for the Lord and sharing Christ with others along my way. I also had periods in my life where I was living in the flesh outside God's will and missed opportunities for God to use me. The important thing was that I had Jesus in my heart, and I had the benefit of the Holy Spirit to convict me when I chose sin over obedience (Ref: Luke 11:13). One of the beautiful things about a personal relationship with Christ is His willingness to forgive our sins (Ref: 1 John 1:9). It is important to know the truths of the Bible and stay on the straight and narrow path.

Every time I stumbled in my spiritual walk, satan was there to use it as an opportunity to pull me further away from God. I gave satan plenty of opportunities, but I also understood God's truth about being His child *forever*. (Ref: John 10:28).

It is hard to understand how God can be so loving and for-giving when I fail Him so often. It is also the most reassuring truth in my life. There are literally hundreds of verses telling me of God's promises to love me, forgive me, and never leave or for-sake me (Ref: Hebrews 13:5-6).

My favorite story, (not in the Bible), relates how I can count on the Lord. It is the "Footprint Story." In the storms of life, I've had one set of footprints many times where the Lord carried me. Through it all, God had a purpose, and I have learned to trust in His timing and His direction.

Without my personal relationship with my Heavenly Fa-ther, I'd be in big trouble. Trying to make my way through this sin-filled world on my own is a scary thought, but that's a storm that no longer tosses me around. I have learned through count-less failures that I am nothing without Christ Jesus (Ref: Psalms 121:1-2). I still stumble and must call on God's promises of for-giveness, but satan doesn't stand a chance; God is on my side (Ref: Romans 8:31).

An Invitation

Today is the day of salvation, my friend, and Jesus is waiting on you to reach out, while you still have time. (Ref: 2 Corinthians 6:2). Don't put off the joy you can have in the Lord yet another day. Christ will come live in your heart if you simply ask Him to!

It need not be anything other than a simple prayer lifted up to Him, with a heart that is truly seeking to walk with God. Man sees the outward appearance, but God sees the heart. If you're not sure whether you will go to heaven when you die, you can know for certain by praying for Christ to come live in your heart today. You can use any words you choose, as long as they are sincere and from your heart to God.

If you're not sure what words to say, use the Sinner's Prayer below to begin a new life in Christ.

> Dear Lord Jesus, I know that I am a sinner and I ask for your forgiveness. I believe that you died for my sins and that you rose from the dead. I turn from my sins and ask you to come into my heart and life right now. I want to trust and follow you as my Lord and Savior, in Jesus' name Amen.

Time Is Short

Time is running out; the final curtain will fall, and Jesus will return. Don't be left in the dark, my friend, the time to run to Jesus is now. Are you ready for His return? Don't be left behind, take a leap of faith today – He will catch you in His arms. Don't put off God's free gift of eternal life one more day.

The Final Curtain

I know most folks don't have time
to contemplate such things,
Yet, each day the end gets nearer,
that's what each new day brings.
Don't spend every waking moment
wondering when the final curtain will fall,
Then again it's probably not smart
if you don't think about it at all.
Some people are afraid to discuss
when the world's going to end
To me it means Jesus will return
and Jesus is my best friend.
We've had many predictions over the ages
but we've never had a close call,
God clearly tells us in the Bible,
no one knows when that curtain will fall.
That hasn't stopped the so-called "prophets,"
Bible scholars, and your average Joe,
From trying to be the one to predict
what God said you can't possibly know.
Somehow we think we know more than God

I'm not sure how we started this trend,
It's certainly not true and we'll never guess,
when the world's going to come to an end.
The real question is not when is Christ coming
but are you ready for His return,
You'll need to get saved and surrender,
and there's a book of truths you should learn.
It's as plain as day if you study the Bible,
Christ will come like a thief in the night.
If you're not sure you're bound for heaven,
friend, it's time to get your heart right.
With each passing day, the end gets closer,
yet we're busy with our own daily grind,
Make sure your heart is right and ready
before there's no time to change your mind.
You may debate well, or you may be a good salesman,
but on that day you won't be able to stall,
Just give your heart to Jesus, my friend,
then you'll look forward to that final curtain call.

Being confident of this very thing, that He which hath begun a good work in you will perform it until the day of Jesus Christ.

Philippians 1:6

Made in the USA
Columbia, SC
28 August 2025

61376570R00207